Thinking About American Higher Education

Thinking About American Higher Education

The 1990s and Beyond

J. Wade Gilley

American Council on Education Macmillan Publishing Company

NEW YORK

Collier Macmillan Canada
TORONTO

Maxwell Macmillan International
NEW YORK   OXFORD   SINGAPORE   SYDNEY

Macmillan Publishing Company
866 Third Avenue, New York, N.Y. 10022

Collier Macmillan Canada, Inc.
1200 Eglinton Avenue East, Suite 200
Don Mills, Ontario, M3C 3N1

Library of Congress Catalog Card Number: 90-20406

Printed in the United States of America

printing number
1   2   3   4   5   6   7   8   9   10

Library of Congress Cataloging-in-Publication Data

Gilley, J. Wade.
    Thinking about American higher education : the 1990s and beyond /
J. Wade Gilley.
        p.   cm. — American Council on Education/Macmillan series on
higher education)
    Includes bibliographical references (p.   ) and index.
    ISBN 0-02-897162-0
    1. Education, Higher—United States—Aims and objectives.
2. Universities and colleges—United States—Administration.
3. Higher education and state—United States.   I. Title.
II. Series.
LA227.4.G55   1991
378.73—dc20
                                                                    90-20406
                                                                        CIP

Contents

Preface

Historically, America has been defined by the continuous search for new frontiers. Similarly, American higher education in the twenty-first century will be defined both by its capacity to seek new frontiers and by its exploration of the frontiers discovered by a science-driven economy.

Important questions face this nation's colleges and universities. In an extraordinary time, will extraordinary leaders emerge? Will institutions be aggressive in defining their futures? Or will they be reduced to asking exotic questions and measuring annual budgets? And what about larger issues facing all Americans? Will colleges and universities join in and help the nation weather its transition to a new era?

This book is about the challenges and issues facing America's colleges and universities as the United States and the world enter a period of great change. The 1990s represent not only the impending arrival of a new century, and the prelude to a new millennium, but also a period of transition into a new economic age—often called the information age or knowledge age. Whatever the name, a new science-driven order has been emerging ever since the publication of Einstein's Theory of Relativity in 1916.

The 1990s will see the fast-paced culmination of this evolution as technology, principally telecommunications, renders communism obsolete and disrupts the social values that have long defined the western world. As we move at an ever-increasing pace toward a new century and a new context for mankind, America and its colleges and universities must simultaneously respond to the lingering effects of a dying era and the bold challenges of a new one.

This book explores three major imperatives that will drive American higher education through the 1990s and into the twenty-first century. First, colleges and universities must respond to six critical challenges: minority participation, financing quality education, replacing quality faculty, affordability, institutional ethics, and national competitiveness. Second, strong leadership is required at both the institutional and state government levels. Presidents of institutions must be willing and able to deal with stronger state mandates on social and economic problems. Governing boards must be willing to focus their attention on strategy and initiative rather than micromanaging their institutions. And, finally, the impact of changing regional economies will transform certain institutions located in burgeoning metropolitan areas and foster new forms of higher education designed to meet the challenges of the twenty-first century.

To identify the critical issues facing American higher education, The Center for Policy Studies in Education (CPSE) at George Mason University in Fairfax, Virginia conducted a comprehensive survey regarding higher education in 1988–89 (see Appendix). Those surveyed included 150 college and university presidents of public and private two- and four-year institutions from throughout the fifty states; the governors of all fifty states; and fifty other higher education leaders, including the heads of all national higher education associations located in Washington, D.C. and a small number of professors. This survey, which identified the six major issues plus other topics covered in this book, was supplemented by information from earlier surveys conducted by the CPSE in 1985, 1986, and 1987–88.

The information and ideas included in this book come from many sources, but predominantly from my own experiences and observations. The chapter by Edward L. Delaney and Donald M. Norris reports on their personal observations of the response of institutions to educational demands in several hypergrowth regions around the country. George B. Vaughan's chapter represents his thoughts based on thirty years as a scholar and community college president. This book was written in nontechnical prose, with a general reader in mind. It is not a research summary, relying extensively on previous works or minute analysis, but rather a book about ideas, reflecting its title: *Thinking About American Higher Education: The 1990s and Beyond.*

Above all else, the exciting century ahead will revolve around ideas. Competing ideas will ultimately shape the agenda for American higher education in the twenty-first century. It is my hope that this book will contribute to that dialogue, and that some of the ideas presented here will help develop a forward-looking context for colleges and universities across the country.

No project such as this evolves in isolation; many people have contributed to this book in one way or another, some without knowing it. Two people, however, have made major contributions: Dr. George W. Johnson, president of George Mason University, through his encouragement and availability on a regular basis to discuss and critique ideas; and Sandra Millers Younger, by providing invaluable assistance in researching and writing the book. Both Johnson and Younger have the heartfelt thanks of the author.

The support of the American Council on Education, through its president, Dr. Robert Atwell, and director of publications and advancement, James Murray, is also greatly appreciated. Without ACE and its affiliation with Macmillan Publishing Company, American higher education would lack a valuable forum for the discussion of ideas and issues.

J. Wade Gilley
Fairfax, Virginia

The Authors

J. Wade Gilley is senior vice president, professor of systems engineering and higher education, senior scholar at the Center for Community College Education, and director of the Center for Policy Studies in Education—all at George Mason University in Fairfax, Virginia. Formerly president of three colleges and Secretary of Education for the Commonwealth of Virginia, Gilley has served as senior vice president at George Mason University for the past nine years. He was the primary author of *Searching for Academic Excellence* (ACE/Macmillan, 1986), and *Administration of University Athletics: Internal Control and Excellence* (ACE, 1986).

George B. Vaughan is professor and director of the Center for Community College Education at George Mason University. He has served as president of two community colleges and is the author of two major works on community college leadership. Vaughan's chapter provides a community college perspective on the issues examined.

Edward L. Delaney and **Donald M. Norris** have for the past two years studied the responses of institutions of higher education to the needs of rapidly and dramatically changing "hypergrowth" regions, including Atlanta, southern California, central Maryland, southern Florida, and northern Virginia. The response of institutions in these regions offers insight into factors affecting the future shape and orientation of colleges and universities. Delaney is assistant vice president and director of institutional research and planning at George Mason University. Norris is vice president of the M & H Group of Boulder, Colorado and heads their Washington office.

1

The Context: Change, American Higher Education, and the Twenty-First Century

Since the introduction of Einstein's Theory of Relativity in 1916, science has exerted an ever-growing force in economic, social, and political change. As the world moves toward a new century and a new millennium, the pace of science-driven advancements has so accelerated that the very idea of change has become a part of virtually every American's consciousness. The American higher education establishment knows and constantly talks about the rapid pace of change, but is it really preparing or adjusting for the requirements of a new age?

EVOLUTION OF A NEW AGE

The new science-driven economy—also known as the information or knowledge economy—began to take shape after the Russians' launch of Sputnik in 1957, when the computer was married to the satellite. This merger of two major and evolving technologies resulted in the creation of the telecommunications industry, a development that has since transformed the world. By 1970, the growing power of science and technology had begun to supplant the old industrial economy with a new information-driven economy. (By coincidence, the industrial economy began dominating the agricultural economy nearly a century before—about 1870).

1

In the industrial economy, "working" machines were used to amplify muscle power; in the information economy, "thinking" machines, i.e., computers, are used to amplify brainpower. Consequently, the value added to products is no longer necessarily due to energy or muscle power, but rather increasingly to brainpower. For example, a substantial part of the value added to iron ore from the ground as it is converted to steel is energy: energy to mine ore and coal, energy to fire furnaces and extrude the steel, and energy to transport the steel to factories or other points of use. The industrial economy was thus devoted to materials—the management of things physical, both people and materials. This was an organizing force of nations and corporations.

On the other hand, the energy necessary to create a new computer program, to transmit that program across oceans and continents via satellites, and to envision its use in operating machines and in other entrepreneurial enterprises requires very little energy. The value added in the creation of computer programming—for Lotus 1–2–3, for a flight simulator, or for an automated factory—may amount to millions of dollars, and is the result of brainpower.[1]

This new order is challenging the idea that certain scarce natural resources limit the world's economy. For example, a microchip, the basic building block of the computer, is made from silicon and aluminum, two of nature's most abundant materials. Consequently, the tiny microchip, which has propelled us into the new era, at the same time epitomizes that era. In the new age of information and knowledge, humankind will not be limited by geographic and natural resources, but rather by ideas and technology. This turn of events carries several implications. Abundant energy may become available from the world's most plentiful resources—the oceans, the sun. But the world's next source of wealth will be brainpower.

ADAPTING TO THE NEW ORDER

The microchip, and microcosm in general, is reorganizing industry and commerce, and even the powers of states and nations. Perhaps this is the reason for the current turmoil in socialist countries. After all, socialism is founded on the idea that people can be organized by factory guidelines—moved around and managed like chunks of ore, pieces of metal, and drums of oil.

The shift from Isaac Newton's notion of materialism to Einstein's notion of microcosm is particularly hard for industries to comprehend. Fundamental changes in economic forces portend sweeping changes in the way people work and a corresponding re-structuring of work force requirements. Further, economic changes are being compounded by changing mores, demographics, and urban organization, and all of these changes are synergistic or symbiotic or both. Disorienting to most people, this web of change is beginning to have an enormous impact on human behavior, affecting families, politics, and social institutions such as schools and colleges.

MORES AND FAMILIES: AMERICA IS CHANGING

Dramatic changes have occurred in American families and mores in the last quarter century. The divorce rate, the percentage of households headed by women, and the number of children living in poverty have all risen significantly. At the same time, the rapid influx of women into the work force, including those from intact families, has changed the profile of the typical American family. Not only do women comprise a majority of students in American colleges, but they are also moving into professions previously dominated by men—law, medicine, and business management.

These changes have triggered a variety of consequences, including a growing number of latchkey children (school children of working parents who return home to empty houses), and an increasing demand for private sector involvement in both community and work site child care centers. Of further concern, more and more children are living in poverty, especially in the inner cities. This phenomenon may signal the emergence of a permanent underclass—a new and frightening development in a nation renowned as the "land of opportunity."

Is the development of a permanent underclass, including a disproportionate number of children living in poverty, a function of economic change? In part one could say yes! Despite the fact that women generally outnumber men in colleges today, women with children generally lack the level of economic skills held by men of the same age. Thus, while the change from an industrial to an information and service-oriented economy has produced more jobs for women, many of these positions are at low wage levels. This tendency has been exacerbated by changing mores and family patterns leading to growing numbers of single female heads of households. Those women with either large families or extremely limited employment skills increasingly find themselves and their children a part of the permanent underclass. This dilemma has generated particular concern in minority communities.

CHANGING DEMOGRAPHICS: A NEW AMERICA
AND NEW AMERICANS

A DIVERSIFIED POPULATION.   America's demographics are also changing rapidly. Immigration is up: some 10,000,000 foreigners came to the United States during the 1980s. Only one other decade in American history recorded this many new immigrants—the years 1900 to 1910, when the country welcomed another 10,000,000 newcomers. World War I cut that wave of immigration short, but current indications suggest the trend of the 1980s will continue, with more than 10,000,000 new immigrants expected to arrive during the 1990s. (This could be particularly true if countries in Eastern Europe continue to move toward more individual freedom for their citizens.)

By far, the largest number of new American citizens in the 1980s have been Hispanics from Mexico and Central and South America. The second largest group has come from Asia, including some 700,000 from Korea. Barring the possibility of significant numbers of Russian Jews and Eastern European emigres or an unforeseen international disturbance such as a world war or a world depression, these immigration patterns of the 1980s should persist through the 1990s.

All of these statistics, plus the current low birthrate among native Caucasians, mean that the American population will continue to ethnically diversify at an increased pace during the 1990s. By some estimates, 50 percent of all American children will be non-Caucasian by the year 2000. A 1989 school census in affluent, predominantly Caucasian Fairfax County, Virginia, for example, reveals that this community of 750,000, just outside the nation's capital, will see Caucasian public school enrollments drop from 75 percent to roughly 50 percent by 2000. In this case, the largest minority population is of Asian descent, followed by African Americans, with Hispanics growing most rapidly. The combined average SAT score in 1988–89 for 8,500 Fairfax County high school seniors was 983, with the following breakdown: Caucasian, 1010; Asian, 958; African American, 820; and Hispanic, 906. If achievement levels among minority groups, including Asians, do not improve dramatically in the next 10 years, the composite SAT average for Fairfax (and Virginia) students could experience a free-fall. This trend holds true in most of the nation's rapidly growing states—California, Arizona, Texas, and Florida—as well as in Virginia. The question is: How prepared will new, diversified generations of Americans be for full participation in the new economic milieu?

AN AGING POPULATION.   Another fact of contemporary American life is the aging of the population. Five workers now provide retirement benefits for each Social Security beneficiary. By the turn of the century, this ratio will fall to three to one. Early retirement programs instituted by local and state governments and the private sector have shifted many highly skilled, late-middle-aged workers to the retirement rolls. This trend, coupled with a significant decrease of young workers entering the job market, will tend to further tighten the future pool of expert labor at all levels.

ECONOMIC DISPARITIES. Disparities among America's economic groups are becoming increasingly significant. The number of upper middle income families ($50,000 to $250,000 annual household income) is growing, as is the number of lower income (less than $25,000) families, while the traditional middle income family ($25,000 to $50,000) is disappearing. (The percentage of wealthy households—$250,000 and up—is holding steady.) Poverty among the elderly (age seventy and older) continues to decrease (only one in ten now), but poverty among children continues to increase (one in three). These trends may be explained by the fact that individuals with college degrees, regardless of race or origin, tend to marry one another and establish more traditional families, while those without a college background tend not to establish traditional families. According to *Futurist* magazine, this trend may produce an educated elite after the turn of the century.[2]

SHIFTING ECONOMIC CENTERS: A NEW URBAN ORGANIZATION

Another consequence of the new science-driven economy is the shifting of economic and population centers. In the industrial economy, ports, national crossroads, energy centers, and rivers often dictated the locations of major economic centers and great cities. The confluence of three rivers and a railroad, for example, made Pittsburgh a national economic hub.

But the new knowledge-based, service-oriented economy is creating new economic centers and a new urban organization. Many new hypergrowth centers of varying magnitude are emerging, including Charlotte, North Carolina; southern California; central Florida; northern Virginia; and central Maryland.

The organization of these new population and economic centers differs significantly from their industrial economy counterparts. The industrial revolution produced elevators, automobiles, and mass transit (street cars as well as railroads), which led to urban areas organized into central city, suburb, and exurb. In the new economy, telecommunications innovations (including facsimile machines) and new transportation challenges have given birth to a new urban configuration commonly called "urban villages," "satellite cities," or "the distributed city."* This phenomenon, found worldwide in post-industrial regions, is characterized by substantial semi-independent yet distinct population concentrations, each including office and research space, shopping and recreational facilities, and residential areas frequently located within close proximity (approximately ten miles).

Northern Virginia, for example, now includes at least eight such concentrations, with more than 10 million square feet of leasable office space each. The largest of these is Tyson's Corner, which comprises 28 million square feet of office space and the largest concentration of shopping/commercial space south of New York City. Some 67,000 people work in Tyson's Corner; 400,000 live within a fifteen-mile radius. Tyson's Corner and the neighboring areas of Reston and the Dulles Airport Corridor—a fifteen-mile-long, mile-wide strip of land—are projected to encompass 100 million square feet of office space, 350,000 jobs, one million residents, and twenty-first century shopping, recreation, and transportation facilities shortly after the turn of the century. A major new American city is being created in this Fairfax County area, just outside the nation's capital.

The term "urban villages" now used to describe such new population and economic centers was popularized by authors Christopher B. Leinberger and Charles Lockwood. Writing in the *Atlantic* they identified five major forces contributing to this new urban organization in America: (1) the shift from an industrial to a service- or knowledge-based economy, (2) the resulting explosion of office space construction, (3) the telecommunications revolution, (4) the lower cost of building office space in the suburbs, and (5) the continued preference of the public for private transportation.[3]

The emergence of these new economic centers has resulted in more impoverished, crime-stricken cities and permanently depressed (or recessed) rural areas. Shifting economic forces continue to generate an uneven economy with many regional disparities. This does not mean, however, that every former economic center or great city is destined for ruin. One only has to look at Pittsburgh, the former Steel City, to see a revitalized older urban center. Pittsburgh's revitalization was built on a foundation of education, led by two excellent universities—the University of Pittsburgh and Carnegie-Mellon University.

---

*The term "urban villages" was coined by Leinberger and Lockwood in an October 1986 *Atlantic Monthly* article, *"How Business Is Reshaping America."*

These fundamental changes in America—a new economy; new mores and family patterns; a diversified, aging population; and the creation of new economic centers present formidable challenges for the nation's educational system, from grade schools through the major universities. Never in the history of the United States has education been more important; never have the challenges to educators been greater.

CHANGE CHALLENGES HIGHER EDUCATION

What do recent changes in the world economy, coupled with internal demographic and social changes, mean for America's colleges and universities? Can an educational system developed for an industrial society really meet the challenges of a very different age? What are these challenges? How can they be met?

ORIGINS OF AMERICAN EDUCATION. The structuring principles of the American educational system originated in a culture fundamentally different from ours; they consequently bear little relevance in a science-driven, information economy. Nearly 150 years ago, pioneer educator Horace Mann returned from Prussia impressed with the organization and discipline of the schools there. Mann subsequently introduced the concepts of class and grade to America. Later, the organizing principles of the Industrial Revolution were applied to this educational format. Course credits, pre-testing, post testing, graduate school, academic departments, land grant institutions, state universities (formerly teachers colleges) and many other aspects of the current system were modeled after Henry Ford's assembly line.

The advantages of the American educational system are clear: compatibility and adaptability from school system to school system, from college to college, from state to state, and region to region of the country have effectively resulted in one educational system with largely interchangeable parts. When families move across the country, children can be plugged into a similar school with similar curricula and activities. In a nation where individual mobility is an important factor in careers and the economy, this factory model for schools—and for American colleges and universities—has proven a desirable characteristic, and one difficult to change.

Another strong point in favor of standardized schooling in the past was that input into the system, in terms of student ability and desire, was sufficiently uniform to override the positive or negative aspects of any particular school or system. Fifty years ago, over 50 percent of eighteen-year-olds dropped out of high school before graduation, reducing student populations to those genuinely motivated to learn. Individual schools could thus diverge widely in per-pupil spending, efficiency and quality, and still one could find it difficult to distinguish between them based solely on the performance of their better graduates.

American schools began to fail when a diversity of cultures, mandated schooling for all, and a corresponding decline in the number of motivated learners all converged on an outmoded system designed to process eager learners rather than emphasize learning. As society has begun to change, resulting in more single heads of households, more children living in poverty, and many communities disrupted by the drug culture, the schools' shortcomings have become increasingly evident. All of this has occurred at a time when education is ever more important for both individual success and national competitiveness.

Thus far, the reaction of school reformers—from former United States Secretary of Education Terrel Bell to anxious state governors—has been to fine tune the present system rather than promote fundamental changes. In addition, teacher unions, having no fear of competition, have vigorously opposed substantive change. And they may be right, considering the lack of imagination and real substance in the recent "reform" movement.

Even the September 1989 Education Summit, chaired by President Bush and attended by governors of forty-nine states plus several United States territories, basically resulted only in a pledge to shore up the existing system. The only possible exception to this status quo mindset was the conferees' endorsement of school choice—an idea that cracks the door for market forces to affect schools in the future.

IDENTIFYING THE CHALLENGES. It is critically important to recognize the challenges facing American higher education in the coming decade as a result of an antiquated public educational system. Perhaps most alarming is the suggestion by a recent Southern Regional Education Board report that unless drastic improvements are made in American schools, fewer and fewer high school graduates will be prepared to succeed in college.[4] If the schools do not improve fast enough, what will colleges do? How will they produce the number and quality of graduates required for America to compete in a tough international economy?

Colleges are also faced with the task of attracting and educating an increasingly diverse pool of students, including racial minorities and older students who may return to college many times during the course of productive careers. The need to keep up with costly new technology, demand for institutional involvement in economic development activities, and the management of fundamental changes in educational requirements and delivery systems presents additional major challenges to all colleges and universities.

Other challenges facing America's colleges and universities in the 1990s include the following:

- The 1990s will see a decline in the number of high school graduates, with only a modest recovery in these statistics expected after the turn of century. While some institutions will rally successfully to meet this survival challenge, many others will struggle to maintain their standards as public schools graduate fewer students prepared for college level work.

- The new economy will make long-discussed requirements for lifelong learning a reality. But will courses and curricula developed for recent high school graduates really be adaptable or acceptable to educated, experienced, middle-aged workers looking for critical skills renewal? What about corporate education and proprietary schools? Or will completely new alternatives emerge from new technologies and new corporate structures? Further, might it not be desirable for existing colleges to limit the range of their endeavors and encourage new alternatives?

- The basic organization of colleges and universities is open to question. For example, knowledge in the new age is increasingly less likely to be organized according to established departments and disciplines. But few colleges have been willing to even chance discussing the relevance of conventional departments in the new knowledge age. In addition, the corporate structure of colleges—from the size, function, and operations of boards of trustees to the selection and functioning of chief executives (presidents and chancellors), to the internal vice presidential structure—may soon be obsolete. While colleges and universities continue to mimic the industrial organization, other knowledge organizations, such as major law firms, research laboratories, high tech companies, and health maintenance organizations, are evolving differently. But there is little evidence of organizational experimentation in American colleges and universities.

- One of the great challenges facing colleges and universities in the 1990s is learning to balance a declining pool of quality faculty with technology designed to enhance the impact of exceptional teachers. Not unlike public schools, colleges and universities are faced with improving quality of teaching and learning in a more complex and diverse environment. But at present, colleges appear to be using technology merely to augment traditional teaching methods. Most computer-aided instruction, interactive television, distant learning, and other attempts to use technology in instruction have enjoyed very limited success. No cost-effective uses of technology in teaching and learning have been reported.

Without question, American higher education is facing a time of uncertainty and tremendous change. Americans as a people are entering an entirely new era, one driven and epitomized by change. Within this context, one could write volumes about the future of American colleges and universities. This book focuses on three pivotal areas of consideration: critical internal issues facing higher education in the 1990s; the interplay of state policies, governors and college presidents in educational leadership; and higher education's response to the challenges of rapidly growing metropolitan regions.

This context chapter, "Change, American Higher Education, and the Twenty-First Century," sets the stage for thinking about these topics within a setting of economic, technological, demographic, and educational changes. In part one, Chapters 2 through 7 address six major issues facing American colleges and universities in the next decade: minority participation, replacing quality faculty, financing educational quality, affordability, institutional ethics, and national competitiveness. In chapter 8, noted community college scholar Dr. George B. Vaughan presents the community college perspective on these issues.

Part two acknowledges the importance of states and state policy in shaping and reshaping of public colleges and universities. The abdication of the deficit-ridden federal government from higher education policy-making during the 1980s coincided with the emergence of a new breed of governors intensely interested in education. Their involvement created a new and challenging environment for institutions and their leaders.

Chapter 9 begins this discussion with a report on tensions between governors and institution presidents, followed in chapter 10 by profiles of four noted education governors from the 1980s. Chapter 11 then identifies and compares states with outstanding public higher education systems.

Good management practices in colleges and universities are outlined in chapter 12, which also recommends the academy as a management model for other knowledge industries. Chapter 13 examines the troubling pattern of politicization in higher education, while chapter 14 concludes the section with suggestions for multicampus governing boards on developing system strategy.

Part three considers two new American phenomena. Chapter 15 explores the emergence of hypergrowth regions as centers of the new knowledge-based economy, focusing on the challenges this rapid growth poses for institutions located at the epicenter. Chapter 16 discusses the distributed university, a developing concept that harnesses the power of technology to distribute educational programs and services to participants in regions of both dense and sparse population. Chapter 17 summarizes previous chapters and presents recommendations for action. Finally, the appendix provides a summary report on the CPSE national survey completed in 1988–89.

PART ONE

Higher Education Issues in the 1990s

American higher education, like the nation and the world, has entered the final decade of the twentieth century in the midst of great change. With the approach of a new century and a new millennium, developed societies are shifting from obsolete, industrial-based national economies to a science-driven, knowledge-based global economy. This economic evolution and the demographic upheaval that accompanies changes of such magnitude promise continuing challenges in the years ahead for all institutions of society—including America's colleges and universities.

These pivotal signs of our times hold special interest for those individuals—college and university presidents, state governors, and other education professionals—who must provide the leadership to move higher education through the 1990s toward the next century. What do these men and women see as the greatest issues and challenges facing the academy in the 1990s and beyond?

To answer this question, in 1988 and 1989 the Center for Policy Studies in Education (CPSE) at George Mason University in Fairfax, Virginia surveyed 150 American college and university presidents representing all fifty states and all segments of American higher education, plus governors of the fifty states and fifty other higher education leaders. The 1988–89 survey followed earlier CPSE surveys of governors and college presidents extending back to 1985.

Survey respondents identified a number of critical issues facing American higher education in the years ahead, including: (1) minority participation in higher education, (2) financing quality higher education, (3) affordable higher education, (4) replacing quality faculty, (5) helping the United States keep its competitive edge, (6) governance and leadership, and (7) improving the public schools. Other issues considered important included assessment and accountability, and restructuring teacher education.

Also identified, as part of several issues described by the respondents, was the broad question of ethics. Many of those surveyed suggested teaching ethics to students, while a few questioned whether or not institutions and their leaders were being drawn into practices and situations not unlike recent, highly publicized compromises on Wall Street and Capitol Hill. Follow-up discussions with a number of prominent educational leaders led to the conclusion that setting a good example might be the best way for colleges to start teaching ethics to students.

The first section of this book is devoted to the top five critical issues identified in the survey, plus the question of institutional ethics. The sixth issue—governance and leadership—is discussed in part two under the title "Governors Versus College Presidents: Who Leads?" While certainly a vital topic, the question of improving the schools has been extensively addressed elsewhere and is not discussed in this book. Though public education and higher education are inextricably linked—schools supply students for higher education, and colleges supply teachers for schools—each arena faces unique problems more pressing than their shared concerns.

The issue of accountability and assessment, mentioned by a number of respondents, also is not addressed here. Higher education leaders generally view this topic more as a short-term rather than a long-term difficulty, and most see the issue simply as a symptom of other, larger problems.

These six issues chapters vary in their approach from each other and from standard educational literature. The challenge of minority participation in higher education is confronted in chapter 2 with a "Marshall Plan" of broad solutions. Though this problem is already well understood, college and university decision-makers still have not demonstrated the will to alter the basic structure of American higher education in search of solutions.

Chapters 3 and 7 present straightforward analyses of the issues of financing quality education and economic competitiveness, plus ideas for exploration.

Chapter 4, on affordability, examines such points as the difference between cost and price to the student, the question of price as a function of marketing, and the role of federally guaranteed student loans in pricing and marketing colleges.

The fifth chapter's factual perspective on the issue of replacing quality faculty includes such considerations as the folly of early retirement programs and the pervasive caste system that discourages bright young prospective academics. This analysis leads to strong recommendations.

Chapter 6, a discussion of ethics, hinges on a series of true stories recounting challenges to institutional integrity in a climate of acknowledged greed. (Names are changed to protect the guilty.) Consideration of these actual circumstances raises questions about leadership by example and the need for an academic code of ethics.

In the eighth and final chapter of this section, Dr. George B. Vaughan, professor of higher education at George Mason University and director of the university's Center for Community College Education, comments on the six preceding topics from the community college perspective. Vaughan's commentary is especially valuable in light of the number and unique importance of these two-year colleges within the structure of American higher education.

2

Minority Participation: Mandate for a Marshall Plan

In the 1988–89 CPSE survey of governors, college and university presidents, and other higher education professionals, minority participation emerged as the top issue facing American higher education during the balance of this century. And no wonder.

By some estimates, nearly half of public school enrollments will be minority children by the year 2025, not only in large cities or southwestern border states, but also across the nation.[1] In the affluent suburb of Fairfax County, Virginia, for example, just outside Washington, D.C., educators predict almost 40 percent minority enrollment by 1996. Even today, this once "white" suburb counts some 38,000 minority pupils—Hispanics, Asians, African Americans, and Caucasian non-English-speaking residents—among its total school enrollment of 130,000.[2]

Despite this escalation in public school minority enrollments, a growing pool of minority high school graduates, and, rising minority enrollments at the college level, overall minority participation in higher education is on the decline. Though the number of minority college students increased by one-third between 1976 and 1986 (due largely to dramatic growth in Hispanic and Asian enrollments),[3] the proportion of most minority groups attending college fell during the same period.

The 1988 report, "One-Third of a Nation," produced by the Commission on Minority Participation in Education and American Life, notes, for example, that the percentage of African American high school graduates who had completed one or more years of college rose from 39 percent to 48 percent between 1970 and 1975, then dropped to 44 percent over the next decade before rising again to 47 percent in 1986, a figure still slightly below the 1975 rate. Compounding the problem, a breakdown of male/female enrollment reveals that fewer African American men are attending college—436,000 in 1986 compared to 470,000 in 1976—while African American women have had steady enrollment rates during the same period.[4] These figures have prompted many experts to predict a damaging social gap between the sexes among African Americans, with consequences for society as a whole.

Meanwhile, the rate of college attendance among Hispanic high school graduates fell from 51 percent to 47 percent between 1975 and 1985, while Native Americans continue to register the lowest high school graduation and college attendance rates of any minority group: only 55 percent complete high school, and only 17 percent of these go on to college.[5]

Native Americans constitute a very small portion of this nation's population, a minority even among minorities. Yet in Alaska, Native Alaskans represent some 17 percent of the population, and their numbers are growing. These demographics present a major challenge to the state's educational establishment, particularly the University of Alaska.

In 1989, the university reported a native Alaskan enrollment of only 6 percent, and that figure is inflated given early and high dropout rates. In addition, most evaluators have reported serious problems with the university's performance in educating native Alaskans; some even called it "disgraceful." On-site observation in the spring of 1990 yielded insight into why this institution is not adequately serving its constitutency.

For the most part, the University of Alaska still operates from other minority models tailored to the educational requirements of African Americans living in urban settings. This dated thinking is detrimental to native Alaskan students. It does not take into account the diversity among native Alaskans nor does it consider implications of the subsistence bush (or rural) culture still prevalent among Alaskans, a culture vastly different from those of African Americans, Asian Americans, Hispanics, and other American minorities.

Another issue hampering the university's ability to educate Alaska's native minorities is the question of access vs. distinctiveness. While the university system is clearly concerned with improving access and performance of native Alaskans, there is a conceptual dilemma limiting this pursuit. The imperative question is whether distinctiveness and access are compatible. The flaw in this philosophy is that distinctiveness is not the same as elitism. An institution can be distinct by knowing clearly what it is trying to do and doing an exceptional job of it. Further, this philosophy assumes that minorities are not attracted by distinctive institutions. In fact, many public universities have experienced sharp rises in minority enrollments as they grew more distinctive. By sacrificing everything at the altar of access, one ignores the power of aspiration.

Native Alaskans display a unique identity and creativity, both in their works of art and in their successful adaptation to a challenging environment. Any successful bridge between Alaskans and traditional American higher education must be rooted in Alaska, and not based on dated, irrelevant models of minority education. Clearly, Alaska's future is linked to its effectiveness in educating its native citizens.

The facts are clear and disturbing: Most minority groups in America—African Americans, Native Americans, and a large percentage of Hispanics—are simply not participating fully in higher education. (Although Asian Americans face special educational concerns and challenges, lack of participation is not among them.) This chapter will focus on a broad set of suggested solutions intended to encourage increased involvement by minority groups not currently participating fully in American higher education.

WHERE DO WE BEGIN?

Before we can talk about solving the problem of insufficient minority participation, however, we must find the point where it starts. This is not an easy task; the issue is multifaceted and expansive, and what happens in one area (fewer minorities entering graduate school, for example) affects other areas as well—in this case, a shortage of minority faculty.

A significant problem is now brewing because insufficient numbers of minorities are preparing for careers in education, particularly as college and university teachers, researchers, and administrators.

The number of minority college students earning degrees in education continues to fall at an alarming rate. Of the 100,000 bachelor's degrees awarded to minority students each year, fewer than 10 percent are in the field of education. And while African Americans once composed 18 percent of the teaching profession in this country, today that figure has declined to 6.9 percent and threatens to drop below 5 percent by 1995. Further, less than 2 percent of all teachers in public schools are Hispanic.[6]

The problem worsens at the graduate level, where colleges and universities must look for new faculty members. Between 1976 and 1985, the total number of African Americans earning master's degrees declined by 32 percent. At the doctoral level the total dropped by 5 percent overall, including a 27 percent drop among African American men. Hispanic and Native Americans showed slight gains in the number of graduate diplomas earned during the same period, but their share of advanced degrees remains low: about 2 percent for Hispanics and only 0.4 percent for Native Americans.[7] Over the past fifteen years, African Americans have earned only 4 percent of total doctorates conferred; they compose only 2 percent of college and university faculty.[8] The number of minority faculty will drop further with the advent of massive faculty retirements expected by the turn of the century (see Chapter 5).

But the question of insufficient minority participation in higher education reaches back further—to declining percentages of African Americans at the undergraduate level. This dilemma, in turn, is exacerbated by the fact that many African Americans and Hispanics do not graduate from high school.

Where do we begin? Obviously, this complex problem must be tackled at every step along the way: High school graduation rates must improve so that more minorities can attend college; once in college, these students need added academic support if they are to graduate; and finally, minority students must be encouraged to attend graduate school, and then enticed to turn their career aspirations toward the academy. To further these goals, all graduate students, and especially minorities, must be seen as more than cheap labor hired to assist full-time faculty. They must be viewed as apprentices being groomed as future college and university faculty members.

THE AFFIRMATIVE ACTION/EQUAL OPPORTUNITY DILEMMA

Some observers contend that American higher education has already tried to address the issue of minority participation in academia through the rigorous affirmative action/equal employment opportunity search process employed during the past fifteen years. But this system is flawed by serious drawbacks, most notably, bureaucratic complexity and subjective screening.

Initiated in the mid–1960s, the "open," "affirmative action" or "equal opportunity" search process was born in response to court orders and federal legislation amid a national movement to bring minorities, particularly African Americans, into the mainstream of

American higher education. But with the establishment of an official search process, it was suddenly considered "un-American," "anti-opportunity," and unacceptable to go directly to qualified African Americans and recruit them for specific positions, despite the fact that colleges and universities had done just that for many years! Of course, there were few African American candidates to recruit in those days, largely the result of an entrenched "old boy" network, which usually turned up well-qualified Caucasian male candidates for any given job.

The push behind integration of university faculties actually hinged on an idea of "fairness" rather than "affirmative action." That is, administrators wanted to cast the search net broadly enough to snare a few African American applicants, but then use a tight enough screen that only "qualified" candidates fell though to final consideration and eventual appointment. This calibrated "screen," in almost all cases, has consisted of a committee, broadly based and now usually including a minority member, that relies upon collective judgment rather than specific objectives to determine standards of quality.

The widely cast net and the concepts of "open" and "fair"—key principles of the contemporary search process—have generated additional procedures, so that, in practice, the search process has become a maze of red tape. At a typical medium-sized university, for example, one can find a score of search committees operating simultaneously, but rarely yielding a single minority appointment. At one school, it takes twenty-two distinct operations to finalize one adjunct faculty appointment, including two passes through both the provost's and the affirmative action office. Though these are extreme examples, it is true that what began as an affirmative action effort, in all of its "fairness," has evolved into an incredible bureaucratic labyrinth.

With the advent of the affirmative action/equal employment opportunity movement, it became necessary to spread faculty search nets across the nation, and to document this effort for future auditors. These requirements were met by advertising position openings, a practice which initially yielded sizable new revenues for newspapers. Eventually, the growing need for educational advertising space spawned the *Chronicle of Higher Education*, an excellent industry news source and idea exchange, largely underwritten by search advertising. More recently, another valuable trade magazine, *Black Issues in Higher Education*, has emerged, also largely supported by search advertising.

This new approach to national searches matured in the 1970s and now typically yields scores, if not hundreds, of nominations or applications for positions in higher education, ranging from housing counselors to university presidents. Usually, half to two-thirds of applicants are totally unqualified for the position they seek. But the rest possess some qualifications, and that is where the collective judgment of the screening committee comes into play. As the field of applicants is narrowed, a comment about "being at the wrong type of institution" or a rumor of "personality problems" will frequently dispatch a candidate to the reject file with no further review. In many cases, minority candidates fail to continue past this point.

At the presidential level, final selection boards have recognized that candidates with "questionable" reputations or unique personality traits tend to be screened out in the early phases of the selection process. Fearing that qualified candidates may consequently be overlooked, many institutions now employ professional search firms or organizations to advise them at different stages of the search process. These firms also insert candidates—many of them well-qualified minorities and women—at the "final list" stage, where they stand a better chance of being selected.

One university uses its own AA/EEO office somewhat like an external executive search organization. In addition to routine paperwork, record keeping, and documentation, this office mandates goals and search procedures, and inserts highly qualified candidates into the search process during the final stages. Using an extensive network, the office constantly seeks out well-qualified minority professionals, keeps their names on file until an appropriate position opens up, and then inserts the candidate into the pool of applicants.

This approach has produced impressive results, including the selection of African American faculty members for four of the university's endowed chairs. The in-house search organization continues to yield well-qualified African Americans and other minorities for junior faculty and university administrative posts, while giving minorities the confidence they need to move forward through the rigorous search process.

INNOVATIONS AT THE GRASS ROOT LEVEL

Even at its best, however, the affirmative action/equal employment opportunity search process is not the answer to staffing America's colleges and universities with even a minimal level of African American professionals. To combat the widespread problem of declining minorities at both the graduate and doctoral levels, many institutions have created innovative programs of their own, designed to entice minorities into graduate school and encourage them to pursue academic careers.

One excellent example of these efforts is the Council for Institutional Cooperation, a joint venture between "Big Ten" schools and the University of Chicago.[9] The program consists of the following elements:

- Minorities Fellowship Program (four years of support for 365 fellows since 1978)
- Summer Research Opportunities Program for Minority Students (ninety-eight "talented" sophomores and juniors in the first year, 1986; 220 students in 1987)
- Conference on Graduate Education for Minority Students (annually drawing some 300 participants from a seven-state region)
- International Studies Fellows Program (for minority students interested in international studies)
- Directory of Minority Ph.D. Candidates and Recipients (published annually to increase professional opportunities for minority graduate students and aid in their recruitment)

These programs are funded by the universities involved, as well as private donors, including the Andrew W. Mellon Foundation, the Lilly Endowment, the W.K. Kellogg Foundation, the John D. and Catherine T. MacArthur Foundation, the Exxon Education Foundation, and the Pew Memorial Trust.

Florida offers another excellent example of a comprehensive program to encourage minority graduate enrollment. A coalition of higher education, political and business leaders, underwritten by financial support from the McKnight Foundation of Minneapolis, established a three-tiered program designed to stimulate minority interest in higher education. The plan included the creation of several community centers, a junior faculty development program, and a McKnight Black Doctoral Fellowship. Although still in its infancy, the program is already showing promising results for the future.

EARLY IDENTIFICATION PROGRAMS

A stellar grassroots innovation, the early identification program offers a beacon of hope for moderate-achieving, but high-risk children. Designed to tackle the national problem of declining high school graduation rates among minorities, particularly African Americans, these programs also combat a decline in college attendance among minority high school graduates.

Early identification is already proving more successful than prior "intervention" tactics. Remedial education, for example, a prominent program in the late 1960s and early 1970s, later suffered a backlash of complaints. Critics charged that spoon-fed minority students seemed to handle college well at first, but quickly faded and sank to the bottom of the class. Few remedial students earned degrees. Another 1970s program sent "counseling vans" into low-income communities in an effort to attract minority students to community colleges. But few students recruited in this manner graduated, and, as federal aid rules tightened in the 1980s (and federal pressure to recruit African Americans eased), this practice lost funding and favor.

The early identification program differs significantly from these earlier attempts at minority recruitment; it literally brings children to the university in the eighth grade. In one of the first of these programs, begun in 1988 at Virginia's George Mason University, fifty minority eighth-graders were selected to spend three weeks on campus during that summer. The students were introduced to campus life; they participated in concentrated classes taught by university and specially selected minority public school teachers; and they enjoyed unique recreational and cultural programs. During the subsequent school year, the fifty students, now ninth-graders, regularly attended events on campus and studied with minority college tutors. As the months went by, the students' performance increased significantly, and they began to voice much higher aspirations for their future.

In the summer of 1989, forty-nine of the original fifty students (one moved away) welcomed fifty newly graduated eighth-graders into the program. The more experienced first group had learned to maximize their time and were eager to coach the new initiates. After tenth grade, these participating students will augment their studies with challenging part-time or summer jobs in area businesses and industry. By introducing these young people to professional and technical work environments, program administrators hope to expand their knowledge of the workplace and motivate them toward ambitious career goals.

The early identification program goes one step further in helping these students secure their goals for the future: after successful completion of the program, they will be guaranteed admission to the university and a scholarship from a private foundation to be applied toward attendance at the college of their choice.

A similar early identification program began in New York state in 1987–88 under the joint sponsorship of the Syracuse City School District and Syracuse University. Designed to encourage college attendance among economically disadvantaged and minority students, the "Syracuse Challenge" invites the participation of all Syracuse eighth-graders. Students and their parents or guardians must sign a nonbinding agreement to fulfill program requirements. Participants are then challenged toward specified academic goals and mentored through structured advising, remedial activities, summer studies and involvement in university events. Students who successfully complete the program—which requires an 85 percent average in college preparatory curricula and an SAT combined score of at least 1,000—are guaranteed admission to Syracuse University and full financial assistance. Over 800 Syracuse students—about half of those eligible—accepted the Challenge in each of its first two years.

David C. Smith, dean of undergraduate admissions and financial aid at Syracuse University, said the program aims to counter a perception among urban minority youth that college is beyond their grasp. "We're going to eliminate the uncertainty," Smith told the *New York Times*. "These students now know for sure that, if they do certain things, they can get a college education."[10]

Familiarity with the campus atmosphere and exposure to professional work environments are proving to be powerful motivators for at-risk minority children. Equally important is the nurturing environment provided by program staff, college tutors, and participating high school and college faculty. The full cooperation of area schools, which provide transportation and contributions, also helps assure the success of these innovative programs. And the local business community plays a vital role, too, by helping to fund the program while introducing young students to new career opportunities and broader educational experiences.

Future prospects for continuing and expanding early identification programs are excellent, but such programs must be multiplied a thousand times across the nation to become an important part of a national effort to encourage minority participation in higher education.

A MARSHALL PLAN FOR THE 1990S

If America is to move toward full minority participation in higher education, we must implement the educational equivalent of the Marshall Plan—the comprehensive strategy that revived a devastated Europe after World War II. Indeed, we can afford nothing less than such an all-out national effort if America hopes to remain a leader among industrialized nations. Without an educated, competitive work force, this nation will begin a sure decline toward second-class economic status, coupled with a diminishing standard of living.

Should that happen, the underclass will grow while the upper class shrinks, pushing the United States toward the two-class society now evident in many third world countries. It may take 200 years for such an imbalance to evolve, but all current signs point toward this frightening scenario. That is why intervention is required, and now! The alternatives—doing nothing or making some halfhearted effort—will surely aggravate the situation as we approach the twenty-first century.

I recommend, therefore, a five-part approach for tackling the problem of insufficient minority participation in higher education.

1. *MORE FEDERAL INVOLVEMENT.* First, the federal government should provide encouragement and incentives for institutions, state, and multistate organizations to come together to address the problem. Further, the federal government should itself focus increased attention on the issue of minority retention. The United States Department of Education should review, reconstitute, and revitalize the twenty-year-old TRIO programs—talent search, upward bound, education opportunity centers, and special services for disadvantaged students. These programs offered much promise (and did much good) as part of Lyndon Johnson's Great Society efforts during the 1960s. In recent years, however, particularly during the Reagan Administration, little has been heard of the TRIO programs. In addition, several federal efforts seem to have lost their bearings, including the Fund for Post-Secondary Education, which has turned into a playhouse for a closed circle of "innovators," with little national direction. Since a dramatic improvement of minority retention in higher education would benefit the national interest, and since states and institutions have already taken the lead in offering solutions, it would only be fair that the federal government be involved as well.

2. *MANDATING A NATIONAL EARLY IDENTIFICATION PROGRAM.* Second, every institution of higher education in America should commit to establishing an early identification program. If every college and university in the nation assisted between fifty and 200 at-risk minority eighth-graders each year (an average of about 100 students per school), the 3,200 American institutions of higher education could serve about 300,000 eighth graders annually, providing an enormous boost to minority participation.

The problem of insufficient minority participation in higher education is so pervasive and critical it should command top priority attention among college administrators. And there is absolutely no

good reason every college in the country cannot fund the basic operating costs for such a program. At an average cost of $100,000 per
program per year, for example, the total national cost for offering an
early identification program at every American college and university would be about $320 million. While this may sound like a lot of
money, it represents a small investment in comparison with other national priorities: approximately one five-hundredth of the national
deficit ($150 billion), one sixtieth of the federal education budget ($18
billion), and one three-hundredth of the national higher education
budget ($90 billion). In fact, $320 million is less than one fifth of the
combined annual marketing and publicity budgets of American colleges and universities!

We need a large and prestigious leadership group—educators,
political leaders, captains of business and industry, and heads of
large philanthropic organizations—to join forces to adopt a national
model early identification program, and then encourage, challenge,
and badger colleges and universities to undertake such a program.
While each college should fund basic operating expenses out of its
own pocket, other community organizations will pitch in and help.
Public schools can help identify students to participate in the program, provide transportation, encourage outstanding teachers to
work in the program, and generally delight in the opportunity to
work with colleges in such an important effort. Local foundations
can help with college scholarships. Area business and industry can
also supply scholarships, plus guest lecturers, tours of facilities, and
summer and part-time jobs.

3. *THE CHALLENGE FOR THE STATES.* I believe we must also begin to
address the problem of insufficient minority participation in higher
education at the state level. Almost every state contains a minority
population; therefore, the states must share in this challenge, especially if we, as a nation, are to attack the significant corollary problems of poverty and national competitiveness.

Without increased participation of minority groups in post-
secondary education, the competency of the nation's work force will
decline as the proportion of minority workers continues to grow.
This phenomenon, in turn, threatens the country's economic position
in the world, and the quality of life at home.

Promising solutions to these national dilemmas can be found at
the state level. Every state should adopt a program like the Mc-
Knight-Florida effort to increase both baccalaureate and graduate
degree production among minorities. Following the example of many
major private foundations, organizations such as the National
Governors' Association or the Education Commission of the States

should also make minority participation a top priority in the coming decade, broadening the search for ways to combat this national problem.

4. *WHAT WE CAN LEARN FROM THE MILITARY*. Statistics indicate minority youngsters are selecting the military over college in ever-increasing numbers. The military's promise of discipline, focused learning, and physical training seems to be much more attractive to minorities than the ambiguity of the college curriculum—or the total college experience, for that matter. By offering a similar experience as a transition between high school and college, American colleges and universities might encourage more acceptance and participation by minority students. One idea would be for each major university (with enrollments of 2,000 or more) to establish its own prep school. Such schools would be tuition-free (federal financial aid could be extended to these prep schools), and in some cases provide residential facilities. Students could take one six-week course at a time; the curriculum would include a heavy focus on study skills, athletics, and discipline. A similar program has already proven enormously successful at Fork Union Military Academy near Charlottesville, Virginia.

5. *SUPPORTING OUR HISTORICALLY BLACK COLLEGES*. Finally, a national plan to increase minority participation in higher education must capitalize upon the resources of historically black schools, which continue to serve one-quarter of all African American college students and produce a significant number of African American professionals. Though the very existence of these institutions came under attack in the 1970s, they have emerged from the 1980s as beneficiaries of a special relationship with both the Reagan and Bush administrations. In the South, state governments grew much more supportive of historically black public colleges and universities during the 1980s than during the preceding two decades.

Now stronger than ever before, historically black colleges and universities have also gained increased support from African American professionals and entrepreneurs, most notably Bill Cosby who donated $20 million to Spelman College in Atlanta. And prominent African Americans from all over the country are once again sending their children to historically black schools. One example is John Slaughter, former National Science Foundation director, former chancellor of the University of Maryland, and current president of Occidental College. Slaughter himself was educated in electrical engineering at the University of Kansas and the University of California at Los Angeles, but his daughter chose to attend Hampton University, a historically black school in Hampton, Virginia.

There is no question as to the need, viability, and future contribution of these historically black institutions. While philanthropists, both black and white, can help build the margin of excellence with their benefactions, the foundation of support rests with the states and the federal government. Maintaining that foundation in the 1990s is a national imperative.

CONCLUSION

The range of proposals here—increased federal efforts in retention, early identification, state efforts to promote minority graduate studies, special transitional prep schools, and renewed support for historically black colleges and universities—suggests a mammoth national effort, a "Marshall Plan" to increase minority participation in American higher education. Simply put, that is what is required to meet a crucial national challenge.

3

Financing Quality Higher Education

The task of financing quality higher education poses a continuous worry for college and university presidents. Recent surveys indicate no issue looms larger in the minds of college administrators, either as a current or future concern.

In the 1985 CPSE survey of university presidents, more than a third of respondents named funding the single most critical issue commanding their attention on a regular basis. When asked to predict crucial issues five years into the future, a third of survey respondents said they expected funding to remain a top concern in 1990.

Later CPSE surveys confirmed the tenacity of higher education's financing challenge. Funding again emerged as the number one worry among college and university presidents in 1987–88 and 1988–89. In the most recent study, which also included state governors and other higher education professionals, financing quality education ranked third overall among "overriding issues facing American higher education as we approach a new century."

Without doubt, the financial status of American higher education will remain an issue of paramount concern in the decade ahead. In fact, economic and societal changes during the 1980s have complicated funding matters, raising the specter of increasingly critical financing dilemmas in the future.

In the 1970s, staggering inflation rates threatened the fiscal stability of American colleges and universities. A lack of state funding increases, plus cutbacks due to economic shortfalls, left many campuses floundering in futile attempts to keep pace with inflation. Though inflation rates stabilized in the early 1980s, the 1982–83 recession triggered more funding cutbacks across the country.

By the end of the decade, however, old worries of inflation and cutbacks yielded to new headaches that persist into the 1990s. Government funding for higher education, once largely unrestricted, now flows less freely and is targeted toward certain government-determined priorities. In addition, the generous private funding of the 1980s may have peaked.

These limitations have, in turn, raised questions concerning affordability, access, and responsibility. With costs of higher education rising faster than the rate of inflation, many colleges and universities are pricing themselves out of the educational market for students of average or below average financial means. Already, some of these schools have faced the tough choice of limiting enrollment in order to cut costs. Meanwhile, more and more is expected of higher education. Bowing to public and governmental demands, colleges and universities are constantly assuming new responsibilities, though struggling to continue funding their original missions.

Administrators consequently find themselves sprinting to keep up with a science-driven society that generates new educational needs at breakneck pace while rendering many former funding sources obsolete. Not surprisingly, they worry that future funding for higher education may be further threatened by continuing fiscal crises and restraints at the federal level. In the 1988–89 CPSE survey, governors and university presidents listed "federal fiscal stability/balancing the national budget" as the most critical challenge facing America in the 1990s, by a margin of two to one over "social problems" (drugs, crime, homelessness, poverty, etc.)

RESTRICTIONS ON GOVERNMENT FUNDING

One way colleges and universities, particularly private institutions, managed to increase their resource base in the 1980s was by raising costs for students who, in turn, relied more heavily on federally guaranteed loans. This dependency on government-backed aid began with the Middle Income Student Assistance Act of 1978, which dramatically increased the availability of federally guaranteed student loans to middle-income families. Now addicted to the student loan habit, most American institutions of higher education, both private and public, instinctively plead for more federally funded student aid as an answer to the affordability question. Many educators and administrators hoped George Bush's self-labelling as "the education president" would open the federal aid door a crack wider. But are these hopes realistic in the face of a staggering federal deficit?

Despite a de-emphasis of the budget crisis during the early months of the Bush administration, independent budget experts foresee a huge crisis in fiscal 1991 if Gramm-Rudman budget targets are to be met.* In the absence of a tax increase, some experts project 10 percent cuts in defense and social programs may be necessary. But even if such drastic measures satisfy Gramm-Rudman requirements, a $64 billion deficit will remain. Clearly, this scenario offers little hope for significant budget increases for any social programs, including higher education.

Further complicating the government funding situation is the growing practice of "targeting" special projects as recipients of any new higher education spending. Allocations once distributed on a merit basis are now subject to favoritism as influential members of Congress wrangle funding for their own constituents. The fiscal 1990 federal budget, for example, includes more than $250 million dedicated to such "pork barrel" projects at selected colleges and universities, plus another $250 million earmarked for the Superconducting Super Collider (SSC) in Texas. Still another federal funding target is the Continuous Electron Beam Accelerator Facility (CEBAF), a $200 million-plus research facility in Newport News, Virginia. While many of these projects may be entirely worthy of funding, other equally or more valid needs go begging for lack of review or advocacy.

State governments in the 1980s began targeting new higher education funds according to state priorities. For example, during the early 1980s, one state renowned for its excellent colleges and universities (one of the top ten described in Chapter 11), restricted new educational funding to either improving faculty salaries or developing controversial high-tech initiatives. As a result, operating funds for public colleges and universities in this state have been frozen for more than seven years.

---

*Gramm-Rudman refers to a 1985 federal law designed to eliminate the federal budget deficit. The authors of the law were Senators Warren Rudman (R-N.H.) and Ernest Hollings (D-S.C.) and then Congressman, now Senator Phil Gramm (R-Texas). Gramm-Rudman set a deadline for elimination of the federal budget deficit, as well as yearly goals toward that end. If Congress fails to meet an anual deficit reduction goal, the president is directed to cut federal spending, across the board and without priority. In practice, Congress has had difficulty living with Gramm-Rudman and has amended it on occasion to postpone the zero deficit deadline. Also, various budgeting gimmicks have been employed to artificially meet annual goals.

NEW AVENUES OF STATE FUNDING: MIXED BLESSINGS

While many traditional avenues of government funding have narrowed, new possibilities for partnering government and higher education have emerged in recent years, particularly at the state level, with varying results.

The idea of eminent scholars funds, which originated in Virginia, has now spread to a score of states. In the Virginia program—brainchild of the late Colgate Darden, former Virginia governor and University of Virginia president—the state matches income from endowments given to "attract and maintain eminent scholars." The combined donations are used to supplement a full professor line (the budget line item for a full professor's salary), thus yielding a fairly competitive salary. For example, a $12,000 endowment income would be matched by $12,000 from a special state account and the total added to a $50,000 full professor line to yield a $74,000 per year eminent scholars line. This basic concept has been duplicated in various forms in other states, especially in the South.

Similar ideas coupling public and private funds have been generated in a number of states to insure a margin of excellence in higher education. These innovations include centers of excellence, funds for excellence, faculty awards, assessment grants, and new funding agencies for research and economic development.

Another state-level funding phenomenon born in the 1980s proved a failure. Sometimes referred to as tuition ratios, this approach attempted to introduce market factors as restraints on college and university spending. Basically, the tuition ratios plan requires students to pay a certain percentage of an institution's educational and general (E & G) expenses. In one state, for example, in-state students are expected to pay 25 percent of per student E & G costs as tuition, while out-of-state students are budgeted at 75 percent, three times the in-state levy. When first introduced, this policy was touted as a way to control costs: by prorating institutional cost hikes between the state and the students, an institution would be motivated to restrain spending in order to remain affordable. In other words, a market factor would force institutions to operate more efficiently in order to hold down costs to students.

But, in fact, the opposite effect has been the case. Those states implementing this policy have been noted for high tuition and fee increases at their public institutions. Because of student access to virtually unlimited federally guaranteed loans, the market principle failed.

Even the most promising of these ground-breaking, state-level funding concepts carries a price tag: increasing governmental control of higher education via broad-based, state-prioritized programs. In addition, despite promising gains in attracting faculty standouts and maximizing research options, these new approaches to funding have done little to finance operating expenses, maintenance and repairs, or salaries for basic complements of staff and faculty. As a result, America's higher education facilities are aging, and, like the nation's outmoded infrastructure and air fleet, becoming cause for long-term concern.

How can the basic quality of undergraduate education (a top issue for the 1990s, according to the 1988–89 CPSE survey) be improved over the long run if equipment is outdated or worn out, if laboratory supplies are scarce, if buildings are deteriorating, if classes are too large, and if young faculty members see little job security or opportunity for advancement? Further, the challenge of keeping up with technological change in the 1990s will require significant investments beyond basic status quo expenditures.

From both Washington and the state capitals, the message is clear: American colleges and universities can no longer rely on government loans and handouts to pay their bills. Institutions of higher education must cultivate alternative funding sources in order meet the challenge of excellence in the 1990s.

PRIVATE DONATIONS IN JEOPARDY

Even the successful eminent scholars concept, which greatly stimulated private giving to public universities during the affluent 1980s, has spawned unintended outcomes. In many cases, institutions have compromised the integrity and efficacy of these programs by awarding endowed chairs to former administrators and long-time professors who do not qualify as eminent or even distinguished scholars. Abuse of this effective funding channel represents a potentially explosive issue that could wreak havoc in American higher education by stifling private funding in the 1990s.

Public universities have enjoyed increasing success during the 1980s in capital campaigns; benefactors have proved increasingly willing to finance a margin of excellence in higher education. If, however, donors find that universities are instead using their contributions to reward longevity or loyalty, the resulting scandal could permanently damage the fund-raising abilities of these institutions, and perhaps even threaten their state funding.

But administrators persist in courting such disasters. In one recent example, a major public university completed a highly successful capital campaign with funding for forty-eight new endowed chairs and professorships. Of the first twenty-six positions filled, however, twenty-two recipients came from within the university. In fact, of those twenty-two in-house awards, eleven went to current or recent administrators. Such practices rob the university of fresh talent and ideas, while jeopardizing future private funding.

AFFORDABILITY, ACCESSIBILITY, AND COMMUNITY COLLEGES

As states struggle to meet the challenge of increasing costs within higher education systems, a net effect of their funding efforts has been limited enrollments at public universities. Consequently, accessibility to public institutions of higher education has become more of a community college function than a four-year college obligation. Even at community colleges, however, state tuition policies have driven up student costs. One state's tuition ratio policy, for example, resulted in a hike in community college tuition from $350 per year to over $700 per year between 1981–82 and 1985–86—a major shift of costs to the students.

In Oregon, government and education leaders confronted a painful choice between accessibility and quality of education in 1987–88, resulting in direct action to limit enrollment at state universities. Oregon Governor Neil Goldschmidt, a graduate of the University of California-Berkeley's law school, wanted to elevate the state's universities to a level of parity with comparable institutions in neighboring Washington and California. But Goldschmidt's good intentions led to a two-year conflict that shook the very foundations of the university system's governance structure.

Members of Oregon's State Board for Higher Education, the governing body of the state's eight four-year colleges and universities, were committed to a three-point system: accountability, accessibility, and quality. But the state's constitutional limits on spending rendered the latter two goals mutually exclusive. Allocating the necessary funds to service great numbers of students and thereby maintain accessibility meant sacrificing proposed expenditures for insuring quality education.

After a long and often public battle, Goldschmidt gained control of the Board in July 1988, replacing members and appointing a new system chancellor who would be responsive to his direction. When Thomas Bartlett assumed the chancellor's office in 1989, his first policy action was to announce an enrollment cutback. The millions of dollars saved were used to fund quality-oriented improvements, including boosts to sagging faculty salaries. In Oregon, the state finally came to the conclusion that limited resources demanded a choice between access and quality in its university system. Oregon chose quality.

Oregon's decision and similar actions in other states, along with most statewide tuition policies, have tended to push less affluent students toward community colleges. Since, in many states, community colleges derive much of their funding from local government, cost burdens for higher education have often been redistributed. In Oregon, for example, if students are redirected to community colleges because of restrictive admissions policies, actual costs of instruction are transferred from the state to local government.

A QUESTION OF RESPONSIBILITY

A major threat to American higher education is the academy's tendency to take on more and more responsibility without the resources to do those new things well.

This problem can easily be seen in the public schools as well. Following World War II, as the nation began to take its schools more seriously, it also began asking them to solve more and more of the ills of society. By 1980 in Virginia, for example, the state's secretary of education discovered that fifty-six different interest groups felt they held ownership in the public school curriculum. These groups promoted subjects ranging from career education to driver education to sex education—all worthwhile topics, but all taking time and money away from the fundamental mission of the schools.

Many such programs, including special education, career education, and vocational education, were initiated by the federal government with the promise of financial support that never materialized. Further, because schools in most states are funded primarily through a mix of state and local funds (with federal funding providing less than ten percent of the public education budget, and that for special federal interests), the states have found it increasingly convenient to pass the cost of federal and state mandates on to the localities. Only recently have the local school districts balked at this practice; in the meantime, this phenomenon has worked to stretch resources too thin and ultimately diminish the quality of American public schools.

Higher education has experienced some of these same frustrations. The 1960s move to open admissions, for example, represented an effort to provide a college education for people who a generation earlier would have been thought unqualified to succeed at a college or university. Consequently, institutions accepted, and are still accepting, these marginal students, despite the lack of extra resources needed to operate the compensatory programs they require. Instead, colleges have taken from already thin budgets in an attempt to provide additional special programs, while keeping other more traditional college efforts on track with reduced resources.

Another example can be found in the community colleges where missions have been continually broadened in response to public interests—again, however, without the appropriate funding. As a result, community colleges endured an agonizing reassessment of their missions in the late 1970s and early 1980s when funds became more difficult to secure.

In the decade of the 1980s, many colleges and universities yielded to temptation by responding to public and political interests with new services and programs—economic development efforts, minority programs, and others—yet without adequate resources to do a first-rate job. The typical result, as in the public schools, was that resources were stretched too thin overall, jeopardizing the quality of the basic program.

Several studies in the 1980s discovered that institutions juggling too many programs and too few resources could prosper by strategically focusing their programs, i.e., by doing a few things well. Obviously, this is an approach that more and more institutions will be required to use in the 1990s as quality issues become more and more apparent. Further, the practice of initiating additional programs without funding is one that must be generally resisted. Taking on more responsibility should not mean blindly and randomly expanding programs faster than resources.

A MANDATE FOR FUTURE FINANCING

In the final analysis, there is no question that financing quality higher education presents a serious and complex challenge in the coming decade. Government and education leaders must face the following facts as part of the higher education funding picture in the 1990s:

1. It is imperative that faculty salary structures are sufficiently attractive to draw and retain superior educators. High quality teaching and research faculty are the key to quality higher education.
2. Quality faculty members require quality support. State-of-the art supplies, equipment, and facilities are crucial.

3. Colleges and universities must keep up with technological change.
4. The trend of new funding targeting at both federal and state government levels will continue well into the 1990s. The days of generous across-the-board increases for higher education are gone.
5. The practice begun in the 1980s of passing an increasing portion of rising costs on to students who in turn rely upon federal loan programs cannot continue in the face of federal budget constraints.
6. Private investment in higher education, which increased along with American affluence during the 1980s, may also have reached its peak. The careful and fully accountable use of private contributions is imperative to maintain donor confidence.
7. Ideas similar to the national service concept of Senator Sam Nunn (discussed in chapter 4), which further expose American higher education to market forces, are likely as we approach the next century.

WHAT CAN COLLEGES AND UNIVERSITIES DO?

In the face of these current funding realities, one thing is certain: those institutions willing to help themselves stand a better chance than those that wait for deliverance. College and university leaders must be proactive in meeting financing concerns, as in other issues.

An overall institutional strategy is paramount in launching a proactive approach to university leadership. Precedents for such an approach emerged during the early 1970s, a time of crisis for many American colleges and universities. The turbulence of the Vietnam era had ravaged many campuses; the draft was draining away many students; inflation was raging; funds were scarce. Institutions tried any number of ideas in an effort to stay alive: two-year colleges converted to four-year; single sex colleges converted to coed. Still, some schools closed.

But some institutions emerged from deep troubles with great vigor. These schools were characterized by a distinctive university strategy, crafted by strong leadership. They had decided it was not good enough to be like everyone else or to try to do a little of everything for anybody. They had decided to risk everything to be unique. Their daring strategy insured their universities' health and broadened their prestige by narrowing the scope of their work. Two successful examples of this approach are Carnegie-Mellon University and Northeast Missouri State University.

Richard Cyert found Carnegie-Mellon in a crisis mode when he took office as president in 1972. CMU was at that time an excellent regional university, boasting a few nationally recognized programs. But it was a troubled institution, plagued by the Vietnam turmoil, uncertain leadership, ambivalent policies, and significant deficits.

Cyert, a CMU faculty member since 1948 and a former dean of the business school, brought a sense of history to the presidency, as well as considerable expertise in strategic management. Shortly after being named president, Cyert wrote a memorandum requesting all departments to draft a plan for Carnegie-Mellon to achieve national prominence. All replies were to be on his desk when he assumed the presidency on July 1, 1972.

From those responses, Cyert shaped a unique academic strategy. Combined with strong financial management and an opportunistic spirit, Cyert's strategy positioned CMU to surpass its status as a good regional school. During the 1980s, Carnegie-Mellon emerged as a major league university.

On taking office in 1972 as president of Northeast Missouri State University, Charles McClain found a once-respected, but declining former normal school (state teachers college) facing an uncertain future. During the next few years, McClain doggedly pursued a twin path of tightfisted budget control and comprehensive annual testing to assure student learning. Not only did McClain and NEMSU emerge among the founders of the student assessment movement, but the university also attracted a flood of new students, plus additional funds from state and federal government and contributions from private philanthropists.

Further, NEMSU earned a Missouri designation as "The State Liberal Arts College." Once teetering on the brink of financial disaster and student abandonment, this university employed a unique strategy to solve both problems and secure a niche as an esteemed institution.

Other schools may now be following the early lead of Carnegie-Mellon and Northeast Missouri State. A recent article in the *Chronicle of Higher Education* reported that many major private research universities are "focusing their missions," aiming for excellence in fewer things. Administrators of these universities are convinced that a focused and distinctive program will yield funds to expand their margins of excellence. Growing enthusiasm for the concept of institutional strategy offers hope that American colleges and universities will be able to finance quality higher education in the 1990s and well beyond.

RECOMMENDATIONS FOR ACTION

This discussion on financing quality higher education in the 1990s yields a set of recommendations for colleges to consider:

- The development of a distinctive and clearly articulated academic strategy will allow colleges and universities to focus available funds on important programs. If well developed, this approach will boost confidence in the institution among students and those who invest in higher education—politicians, corporations, and families of students.
- Private endowments must be used wisely to advance the margin of excellence; to reward deserving, but needy students; and to move the institution toward distinctiveness. Colleges and universities that use private investments for suspect activities, such as paying off cronies, will almost certainly reap the whirlwind.
- Institutions must set their prices in relation to actual costs, not marketing considerations or guaranteed student loan opportunities. Reports of artificially inflated prices based on the availability of student financial aid will rankle the public. On the other hand, student fees clearly targeted toward quality features are generally supported and encouraged by students.
- Finally, colleges and universities can claim a great reservoir of good will in the hearts and minds of Americans who still believe a college education is the path to the good life for themselves and their children. Yet this positive attitude is not translated into all the federal and state appropriations college leaders insist are necessary. Is this due simply to competition for limited resources or a public impression that colleges and universities are "doing quite well, thank you?" Whatever the reason, colleges and universities must realize it is their obligation to earn and re-earn the trust and support of the public. This is the role of a semiautonomous institution in a pluralistic, democratic society.

In conclusion, there is no question that financing America's colleges at a high quality level is necessary to meet the challenges of a science-driven, education-intensive age. Securing adequate and continuous funding to meet these needs will remain a major priority in higher education for the 1990s.

4

Affordable Higher Education

During the 1980s, the endowment of a respected, private Southern university increased from less than $90 million to more than $250 million. Yet, during this same period, total costs for tuition and fees and room and board rose by more than twice the rate of inflation—to more than $14,000 per year by 1989. Though this university boasts that the median family income of its undergraduates approaches $90,000 annually, 2,390 of its 2,500 undergraduate students receive some form of financial aid.

On June 1, 1989, United States Secretary of Education Lauro F. Cavazos announced new federal regulations governing student loan defaults, which had increased beyond all reasonable limits by 1988. Effective January 1, 1991, the government will limit, suspend, or terminate from the Stafford Loan Program institutions with default rates above 60 percent. Institutions with default rates between 40 and 60 percent will face similar penalties unless they reduce their default rates by 5 percent per year. Higher education officials in Washington declared the new regulations "tough but fair."

Former United States Secretary of Education (1985–88) William Bennett received overwhelming condemnation from the nation's higher education ranks because of his unrelenting attack on the rapid rise in college costs. According to a September, 1988 report in the *Chronicle of Higher Education*, Bennett left office with mixed reviews. Observers credited him for raising the Education Department to prominence, but blamed him for alienating lawmakers and educators with his confrontational approach. Many college administrators considered Bennett's criticisms exaggerated and his proposed solutions simplistic, especially in the area of college costs.[1]

These references raise some unsettling questions. Are college costs rising so fast that higher education is skyrocketing out of reach for many, perhaps most, Americans? If this is true, why are costs rising? Can they be contained? If efforts to contain these costs prove inadequate to keep higher education affordable, what other responses, individual and collective, are available to Americans? And is this a passing issue, or one that will continue to loom on the horizon during the decade to come?

The 1988–89 CPSE Survey of Higher Education indicates that ensuring affordable higher education will remain an issue of paramount concern for American colleges and universities (and indeed the American people) during the 1990s. Governors, college and university presidents, and other higher education professionals participating in the survey named "affordable higher education" one of the top four "overriding issues/problems facing American higher education as we approach a new century." Further, governors and education professionals viewed "affordable higher education/costs to students" as the number one higher education issue in the 1990s. College and university presidents listed it as number four, behind "financing quality," "minority participation," and "replacing quality faculty."

In fact, these four top issues are linked. Affordable college costs and access to student financial aid have long been considered crucial factors in enabling minorities to participate in American higher education. (Minorities represent a disproportionately high percentage of lower income groups and often lack family histories of college attendance.) In addition, college and university officials argue that the recent increases in college costs are a function of "financing quality education," explained by faltering state support and deferred expenses during the hyper-inflation of the 1970s. And, of course, the issue of "replacing quality faculty" carries significant cost implications. Thus, it's not surprising that all groups surveyed listed these four related issues as overriding concerns facing American higher education in the 1990s.

THE COST OF HIGHER EDUCATION

Between 1980–81 and 1986–87, the cost of attending private college in the United States rose by 41 percent, while public college costs rose 22 percent. But during this same period, the average American family's income rose only 5 percent, with disposable personal income rising 15 percent. All four figures are inflation-adjusted; they represent increases in real dollars.[2]

It is clear from these statistics that the cost of attending American colleges and universities is rising much faster than both the pace of inflation and the income levels of average Americans. Further statistics indicate this trend will continue into the 1990s.

Recent projections warn that a year at a private college costing $12,000 in 1988 will total $34,252 by the year 2000. Similarly, a year of study at a state university costing $5800 per year in 1988 will escalate to $16,555 by the end of the century.[3] These figures assume that college costs will rise by six percent annually. If, as College Board policy analyst Janet Hansen points out, average family incomes keep pace with these increases, the college burden may be no heavier in ten years than it is today. But, Hansen adds, during the 1980s college costs increased at a much faster rate than inflation or family incomes. If the rise in college costs in the 1990s continues the rapid escalation of the past decade, college costs for the average American family in the early twenty-first century will approach astronomical proportions.

This view of the future is shared rather broadly. Survey results reported in February, 1988 indicated that influential business leaders, government officials, and journalists see "the rising cost of college to be a major concern." That poll, sponsored by Cornell University and conducted by the Yankelovich organization, also revealed that 31 percent of government leaders were "very worried" about a lack of minority participation in higher education. They were also alarmed by "inadequate financial aid for college students." Further, the survey indicated journalists were skeptical of claims made by higher education officials and tended to support former Education Secretary William Bennett in his criticisms against higher education.[4]

Another 1988 survey by the Gallup organization, sponsored by the Council for the Advancement and Support of Education (CASE), found almost half (48 percent) of 1,000 high school juniors, seniors, and recent graduates who did not go on to college cited price as the key deterrent to college attendance. The poll also found that while one-fourth of respondents said they didn't have enough money to attend college, they generally overestimated college costs by as much as $2,300 per year. Another 33 percent of students surveyed thought most college financial aid is set aside for minority students.[5]

Making higher education affordable is an issue of vital concern to our nation's leaders as well as to educators. President George Bush, in his 1988 position paper on education, vowed that "no student [will be] deprived of a college education for financial reasons."

HIGHER EDUCATION'S RESPONSE

The picture appears grim. College costs are rising rapidly—much faster, in fact, than inflation, family income, or personal disposable income. High school students see these increasing costs as a deterrent to attending college. Influential government, business, and media leaders are worried about the ramifications of escalating college costs. And national leaders, including former Secretary of Education Bennett, have blasted colleges for adding to higher costs through mismanagement.

The higher education establishment has responded to these perceptions and charges by contending that college is still affordable, that rising college costs are justified, that the federal government must provide greater financial support for higher education, and that alternative ways of financing the cost of college must be developed. (Few, if any, college groups or individual higher education leaders have proposed ideas for cost/expense containment at the institutional level.)

In fact, a 1989 survey by Research Associates of Washington (D.C.) found that public higher education remained essentially as affordable in 1988 as in 1978. As a percentage of family income (assuming both husband and wife are in the paid labor force), tuition at public four-year colleges rose less than one percentage point over the decade (from 2.9 percent to 3.3 percent), representing an increase of approximately $100 per year. "With students paying only about one-fourth the operating costs at state institutions, a public education is a tremendous buy," concluded Kent Halstead, author of the report.[6] Further, a 1988, article in the *Chronicle of Higher Education* carried the following headline: "State College Officials Call Public's Panic over Fees Needless." Those interviewed for the story—state higher education employees—pointed out that "more than three-quarters of all college students attend public colleges and universities and pay relatively low tuition."[7] And some state officials, including Gordon K. Davies, executive director of the Virginia Council of Higher Education, think fears over tuition are mainly a "perception problem."[8]

WHY COSTS ARE ON THE RISE

College and university representatives justify the recent rapid escalation in college costs by citing increased budget demands: competing with the private sector for a declining pool of qualified faculty; introducing and updating technology on campus; repairing and restoring college facilities; and increased recruitment and marketing costs. Another justification cited is a shortfall in other revenue sources, including dwindling state and federal support, and declining enrollments, which limit an institution's ability to enjoy economies of scale.

Certainly, any prospect of containing college operating costs must include consideration of payroll expenses: the largest expenditure of any college or university is most likely to be faculty salaries. Unlike other industries dependent on the purchase of raw materials and other commodities, the labor intensive nature of higher education typically requires 70–90 percent of budget allocations for personnel expenses.

Controlling faculty costs will become increasingly difficult in light of impending faculty retirements and the subsequent need to replace many faculty members, plus the dwindling numbers of new doctorates awarded each year. As discussed in Chapter 5, many institutions may soon find themselves embroiled in bidding wars with other schools over a limited supply of well-qualified faculty candidates.

Further, a declining pool of qualified people in certain areas such as science, engineering, and business, will force colleges and universities into increasingly costly competition with the private sector. Quite possibly, this competition for highly educated professionals will intensify in the new "information" economy, triggering a further rise in faculty cost.

Another escalating cost encountered by college administrators is keeping up with the rapid expansion of knowledge and technology. Library books and materials, computers and scientific equipment, and various instructional materials and supplies must be continually updated. To operate even close to the cutting edge of knowledge, colleges and universities must embrace a foresighted investment strategy.

Then there is the cost of deferred maintenance, largely a holdover expense from the 1970s when inflation, high energy costs, and declining federal investment in college facilities forced institutions to defer building and infrastructure maintenance. Obviously, the long-deferred task of repairing and renovating the nation's campuses is critical for continued efficient and safe operation of colleges and universities.

Finally, the push to recruit more students from a dwindling college-bound population is forcing higher education to market its institutions, and at considerable expense. Some institutions, for example, in an effort to impress and lure potential students, have built elaborate admissions centers, not unlike the posh visitor centers often located in commercial or residential developments. Other colleges are now offering scholarships as a marketing tool, with funding from the annual budget. As competition for students continues to grow in the coming decade, marketing will become an even more significant expense for colleges and universities.

COLLEGE TUITION REBATES: THE CATCH 22

In the push to develop marketing strategies for attracting new students, many institutions find themselves in a catch 22 situation. Take, for example, the university mentioned in the introduction to this chapter. Despite its median student family income of some $90,000 per year, its tuition rates have continued to escalate, and nearly all of its undergraduates receive financial aid. How do we account for this situation?

In one sense, costs of private colleges have become synonymous with quality. Price, therefore, can be an important marketing tool. Rather than lowering costs, these schools reserve part of their increasing tuition income to offer "scholarships" for nearly every student, plus extra support for minorities, athletes, and other special admissions. The overall plan constitutes a type of rebate reminiscent of an automobile dealer's sales tactics.

Thus, Secretary Bennett was wrong about the escalating costs of college. Rather than representing a simple case of unchecked operating expenses, increased college costs play a role in a complex marketing/scholarship/minority recruitment strategy that may now have careened out of control. Is it fair that middle-income students borrow huge sums to pay hefty tuition bills, then emerge from college under a heavy load of debt, in part to provide grants for minority or low-income students? One cannot help but wonder about the ethics of effectively taxing a fraction of a generation over many years in order to provide opportunities for the neediest of their peers. Shouldn't the cost of increasing college opportunities for minority and low-income students be the responsibility of all Americans? What will be the long-term effects of this massive borrowing binge? Will the huge loan defaults now already occurring in a small number of private schools expand to become an acceptable way of dealing with college loan debt? Could such a development spread to other forms of personal debt, making bankruptcy a common way of erasing automobile loans and credit card balances? If so, the unintended ramifications of current student loan programs could have a cataclysmic effect on the national ethos.

THE ROLE OF THE FEDERAL GOVERNMENT

The most talked about solution to the affordability dilemma by the higher education establishment has been increased federal grants and loans. In recent years, specifically the Reagan years, education experts have continuously criticized "cuts" in federal student aid.

This early criticism was not unfounded. Reagan's attempts to slash various federal programs included dollar cuts, the implementation of restrictions on guaranteed student loan eligibility, and the removal of interest rate subsidies, forcing students to borrow at market rates. But even a dramatic increase in federal aid would provide only a partial solution to the affordability dilemma, while ignoring a larger issue: controlling the pricing of higher education. Still, the hue and cry for more federal assistance continues.

In 1988, higher education officials met with the House Education Appropriations Subcommittee to ask for continued federal support for student aid and for increased grant aid "to needy students to reduce their reliance on loans." The group, assembled under the American Council of Education umbrella, recommended significant increases in a broad range of federal student aid programs. Richard Traina, president of Clark University in Massachusetts, pleaded for additional federal funding, noting that "educational opportunities for needy students are diminishing."[9]

A PORTRAIT OF FINANCIAL AID

Recent statistics reveal a shortfall between financial aid and the rapidly rising costs of higher education. In 1989–90, financial aid programs in America totalled nearly $28 billion[10] for approximately 12,000,000 full- and part-time students in some 3,000 institutions. The nation's 6,000,000 full-time students received an average of $4,700 per student in federal financial aid.[11] In addition, state spending for aid to needy students was estimated at $1.5 billion in 1988–89. Seventy-eight percent of state financial aid funding went for grants to needy undergraduates.[12]

But a *Chronicle of Higher Education* article, "Fact File: Trends in Student Aid, 1980–81 to 1987–88," indicates that hikes in financial aid during those years amounted to only a modest overall increase when adjusted for inflation (see table 4.1).[13]

Table 4.2 details by source the total number of student-aid recipients awarded in the years 1980–81 and 1987–88. It should be noted

T A B L E 4.1. *Student Aid, 1980–81 and 1987–88*

	1980–81 (BILLIONS)	1987–88 (BILLIONS)	% Change
Federal Total	$14.376	$18.442	+28.3
(Federal Total, 1982 dollars)	16.022	15.37	− 4.1
State Grant Programs Total	.801	1.54	+92
(State Total, 1982 dollars)	.893	1.284	+43.8
Institutional Aid	2.06	4.565	+122
(Institutional 1982 dollars)	2.296	3.805	+65.7
Total Aid	17.237	24.547	+42.4
(1982 dollars)	19.21	20.459	+6.5

that many students, especially the most needy ones, receive more than one award.

The statistics noted above reveal that 46 percent of all undergraduates in American colleges and universities receive financial aid. Total financial aid increased moderately in real dollars between 1980–81 and 1987–88 (up from $19.210 billion to $20.459 billion total aid from all sources in 1982 dollars). Thus, the following figures, for the years 1980–1981 to 1987–1988, represent an overall picture in *real dollars*.

Change in financial aid: +6.5%
Change in costs, private institutions: + 41%
Change in costs, public institutions: +22%
Change in family income: +5%
Change in disposable personal income: +15%

In short, a growing gap exists between costs of higher education and available funding sources—both public and private —to close that gap. The question is, how can this gap be bridged? The following are some ideas currently under consideration and testing.

**T A B L E   4.2. *Number of Student-Aid Recipients,
1980–81 and 1987–88***

	1980–81	1987–88	% Change
Pell Grants	2,708,000	2,862,000	+5.7
Supplemental Educational Opportunity Grants	717,000	660,000	–7.9
College Work Study	819,000	738,000	–9.9
Perkins Loan	813,000	814,000	nc
Stafford Student Loans	2,904,000	3,548,000	+22.2
Supplemental Loans	0	611,000	—
Parent Loans	1,000	176,000	+17,500.0
State Grants	1,140,000	1,580,000	+38.6

INCREASED FEDERAL AID

The higher education establishments, along with leaders in Congress, are gearing up to mount a new drive to increase federal funding for student aid, especially for the most needy students. By every indication, they now have a more sympathetic ear in the White House. But under the shadow of a huge national debt growing by $100 billion a year, plus budget deficits, valid questions persist as to where additional federal money for higher education will be found.

The 1988–89 CPSE survey demonstrated a nationwide concern over the deficit among leaders of higher education. When governors, college and university presidents, and others were asked, "What are the most critical challenges facing America in the 1990s?" their overwhelming response was "federal fiscal stability and the budget deficit."

In fact, of the top three issues cited by survey respondents, concern over federal financial matters outranked the number two issue—"educating the average and less advantaged to fill the needs of business/society"—by three to one, and the third issue—"reverse the growth of poverty"—by four to one.

No one questions the serious national implications of poverty or the need for educated workers in maintaining a competitive work force. Both issues hold critical significance for the survival of this nation. Yet, in the minds of governors, college and university presidents, and other higher education professionals, these two issues do not compare in importance to the problem of "federal fiscal stability and the budget deficit."

In light of these current fiscal limitations, it hardly seems likely that federal funds will be available to tackle the issue of affordable higher education before the mid–1990s. In fact, if a major recession hits the nation's economy in the early 1990s, current federal capacity for student assistance could be diminished. In the short term, however, hope remains for modest increases. And, depending on the economy, larger amounts of federal aid may be possible by the mid–1990s.

SAVING FOR COLLEGE

The idea of saving for a child's education is not new. In earlier generations, upper-middle-class families whose children were expected to go to college began planning well in advance. And some working class parents put aside a few dollars each week for years in order to send a child to college. Even into the 1970s, some parents bought whole life insurance policies on their young children with the idea of later using the accumulated cash value to help finance a college education.

But in the 1960s government student aid programs were established to assure broad access to higher education, and American families began depending on government assistance to finance college costs. As the post-World War II "baby boom" children began coming of age and rates of college attendance expanded dramatically, the nation faced an enormous question regarding access to colleges and universities. In response, states created low-cost, local commuter colleges, including community colleges and urban universities. At the same time, responding to Russia's launching of Sputnik, the federal government in 1958 passed the National Defense Education Act, which contained new student aid programs. Federal assistance to students grew markedly under the "Great Society" initiatives of the 1960s. Though these new government intervention programs succeeded in broadening access to higher education, they also removed the incentive for middle- and lower-income parents to plan or save toward their children's college costs.

Only in recent years has saving for college reemerged as a viable alternative to student loan programs. Now a popular notion, the savings concept is finding its way into public policy and individual planning. College prepayment plans, for example, seem to be gaining a foothold on the state level since they were first initiated in the mid–1980s by Calvin College in Michigan and Pittsburgh's Duquesne University. Duquesne's plan allowed alumni to begin making payments on behalf of a child in return for guaranteed tuition fulfillment by the time the child enrolled. But the concept failed to spread among individual institutions (even Duquesne has since suspended new enrollments in its plan due to "economic conditions")[14] Several states, however, have picked up the prepayment idea.

The first state to launch a comprehensive prepayment program was Michigan, which in 1986 created the Michigan Education Trust (MET) within the state treasury department. The Trust sold advance tuition payment contracts to those who qualified. A year later, this idea spread to Florida, Indiana, Maine, Tennessee, and Wyoming. Other states are now pushing forward with variations on this idea, including tax-exempt savings bonds or accounts at both the state and federal levels.[15] Illinois introduced the nation's first college bond sale in 1988; parents bought $9 million worth of tax-free $5,000 bonds.[16]

NATIONAL SERVICE:
A NEW ANSWER TO AFFORDABLE HIGHER EDUCATION?

Another possible solution to affording higher education is now under consideration in Washington, where congressional leaders, including influential Sen. Sam Nunn (D-GA) and Rep. Dave McCurdy (D-OK), have introduced a bill that would link compulsory national service to student aid. The basis of the Nunn/McCurdy approach would be to phase out current student aid programs in favor of service vouchers of $10,000 for each year of military or other national service. These vouchers could then be used for college tuition, vocational training, or as a down payment on a house.

Nunn's motivations seem to include three major considerations: concern for military manpower in the face of declining demographics; the value of national service to the individual and the nation; and the clear need for a new approach to making higher education broadly affordable.

The concept of national service offers students new hope in the struggle against soaring college costs. Two years of service would provide young adults with broadened horizons and a chance to mature after high school, possibly leading to better academic performance at the college level. And assuming national service programs became popular options for high school graduates, students would not feel "left behind," since many of their peers would also be delaying college. Further, the national service concept could provide an answer to the thorny task of controlling the cost of higher education by bringing market forces to bear on college pricing: students may well begin shopping for value when spending their own resources rather than the deceptively "easy money" of government loans.

POSSIBILITIES FOR THE FUTURE

Obviously, there is no panacea for the challenge of affordable higher education in the 1990s. The next decade will most likely force continuing examination of operating costs for colleges and universities in order to make higher education more affordable for students. Unless institutions act to control pricing and otherwise ensure affordable education, the 1989 antitrust suit may be only the beginning of more serious government charges and investigations.

At least one result of heightened interest in the issue will be a comprehensive search for alternative ways to fund a college education. Along the way:

1. Cost containment will probably become a hot issue in the 1990s, triggering much self-examination among colleges and universities as they attempt to curb operating expenses.
2. Universal national service in some form may become a reality over the next decade.
3. Disenchantment with student loan programs looms as a definite possibility by the mid–1990s as the liberal loan program of the 1980s is seen to cause major negative effects on the national character.
4. Federal student aid will enjoy a modest revival in the early years of the Bush administration, but later face a serious challenge from the national service movement.
5. Saving for college is back in vogue and will be accelerated by state and federal incentives in the 1990s.
6. The practice of integrating student aid into college marketing and recruitment efforts will ultimately break down as marketing efforts reach a point of diminishing return.

The cost and financing of college is beginning to resemble two other national concerns: health care quality and the savings and loan crisis. Like the health care industry, higher education is constantly challenged by the public to become both better and more accessible. Yet states cannot provide more resources to pay for these refinements, and students must not be charged more. As in the S & L predicament, federally guaranteed student loan balances are accumulating into alarming amounts, tens of billions of dollars. These circumstances ensure that the financing of American higher education, i.e., who pays, will undoubtedly mature into a major issue for the 1990s.

5

Replacing Quality Faculty

In 1987, one of the world's leading scholars, a faculty member at an East Coast university, reached sixty-five years of age. Although he was not required to retire, and despite his institution's best attempts to persuade him to stay, he decided to forego his $100,000 salary and retire anyway.

And who could blame him? This professor had options. He could draw a handsome annual pension of $49,500 per year. Better yet, a university in the Southwest had offered him a new position at an additional $100,000 per year!

The scenario of two major universities competing to hire a sixty-five-year-old professor is a relatively new phenomenon in American higher education, but one sure to become commonplace in the 1990s and into the twenty-first century. The reason is simple. The American professoriate is aging at a time when college enrollments are on the rise and the pool of new doctorates is decreasing.

In the 1988–89 CPSE poll of governors, college and university presidents, and others familiar with American higher education, the issue of "replacing quality faculty" ranked second overall (just behind minority participation) among critical concerns facing American higher education as the new century approaches.

The looming faculty shortage is an issue that received little public attention until 1986 when Howard R. Bowen and Jack H. Schuster published their book, *American Professors: A National Resource Imperiled.* Bowen and Schuster concluded that 500,000 new faculty members will be needed over the next twenty-five years as most of the current professoriate, now some 700,000 in number, retire.[1] The *Chronicle of Higher Education* confirmed in January, 1989, that, "by most estimates, more than one-third of the nation's faculty members are older than 50, and many are expected to retire in the next 10 to 15 years."[2] Further, neither of these estimates takes into account the numbers of faculty who will leave academia to seek more lucrative careers in law or business.

The severity of this problem has not yet penetrated the consciousness of American higher education. In fact, many colleges and universities offer retirement incentives to encourage faculty turnover and fresh input from new scholars. Bowen and Schuster were critical of this trend toward early retirement programs, which favor full retirement at fifty-five years of age and thirty years of service. In other cases, early retirement packages are coupled with attractive buyout offers. But in the push to ease out older professors and make way for a new generation of scholars, few leaders in higher education have come to terms with the fact that there may not be enough qualified individuals to replenish the current faculty corps. Indeed, the proportion of doctorates awarded to United States citizens as compared to international students has declined from 85.6 percent in 1962 to 72.3 percent in 1986, according to the National Research Council. Further, in technical areas such as mathematics, computer science and engineering, only one-half of all doctorates are awarded to United States citizens.[3]

These figures have sparked studies by the Consortium on Financing Higher Education, the United States Department of Education and the National Endowment for the Humanities, among others. In addition, the Association of American Universities has commissioned a national research project to investigate the condition of doctoral education in the United States.[4]

CONCERN FOR THE TEACHING PROFESSION

At the same time higher education leaders are anticipating a shortage of college and university faculty, several other issues relating to college faculty have emerged, leading to serious and widespread concern for the teaching profession.

High on the list of these worries is the question of faculty quality in the 1990s and beyond. Higher education is now beginning to receive the level of scrutiny focused on public schools in the wake of "A Nation at Risk," the scathing 1983 report by then-Secretary of Education Terrel Bell. Student evaluations continue to play a vital role in the process of assessing faculty performance, but there is a growing emphasis on elementary instructional materials and self-evaluation, both of which have proved to be valuable tools in improving teaching.

In addition, technology will increasingly be used to objectively evaluate the teaching process, both to measure how much students are learning, and to assist in the learning process.

Concern is also growing about teaching skill levels among faculty. Consequently, faculty development programs are on the rise, as are the numbers of research studies and books on improving postsecondary teaching and learning. Forty-four percent of four-year institutions report some type of formal faculty development programs,[5] and an increasing number of foundations and research centers are also involved in meeting this need.

One example of a professional development program for college faculty can be found at the Center for Community College Education in Fairfax, Virginia. Jointly sponsored by the Virginia Community College System and George Mason University, the Center is dedicated to improving community college teaching by offering a new doctorate, the Doctor of Arts in Community College Teaching. Through this program, the Center is working toward the long-term goal of increasing the number of specially prepared community college faculty in the Virginia system, which faces huge retirements in the 1990s. A program with similar goals is now being established at the University of California at Berkeley. These innovative efforts mark a departure from past community college programs, which focused on helping college administrators find faculty among high school teachers and disgruntled university faculty frustrated by an institution's research demands.

COMPETING FOR QUALITY FACULTY

In the dawning era of competition among institutions for quality faculty, it has now become fashionable for universities to compete for notable faculty as they do for star athletes. This phenomenon of colleges raiding colleges for leading faculty experts has college presidents shaking their heads.

"We've entered the era of the free agency," commented Michael I. Sovern, president of Columbia University.[6]

Sovern's remark was an obvious reference to recent professional sports bidding wars over a few highly desirable star players, a practice born in a climate of league expansions leading to a dilution of overall player quality. Could it be that concern for overall faculty quality is one reason colleges and universities are willing to pay extraordinarily large salaries to a few faculty "stars?"

Just a few years ago, for example, the University of Texas set out to lure Nobel Laureate-class professors with promises of high salaries and exceptional working environments. In an overt effort, the university used booming endowments to pursue these outstanding scholars. Though Texas has been less obvious in its faculty recruitment efforts of late, its early success in attracting big-name physicists to the university certainly played a role in the state's winning the Superconducting Super Collider (SSC), with its accompanying huge economic payoff.

Elsewhere in Texas, the University of Houston won a bidding war with the University of California at Berkeley and retained acclaimed physicist Paul C.W. Chu. Houston's victory came after city boosters raised the money to offer Chu $150,000 per year (three times the average salary of other Houston professors) and a new facility, the Texas Center for Superconductivity.[7] Berkeley, despite the lure of facilities and sentiment (Chu's father taught there), could not match Houston's complete package.

ATTRACTING FACULTY STARS

Boasting of a "big name on campus" has gained popularity as a faddish way to attract attention and improve the marketability of a college or university. "Big names" are usually temporary faculty members who teach one class for one semester, lending more presence than a guest lecturer, seminar leader, or evening class notable of the past. Big names are frequently highly paid. Jihan Sadat, for example, widow of the late Egyptian president Anwar Sadat, was reportedly paid $75,000 per semester to teach one course, plus other duties at the University of South Carolina in 1983 and 1984. Sadat moved on to the University of Maryland where she was paid an almost equally attractive salary of $50,000 per semester.[8]

Other big-name, high salary, one-term professors have included former President Jimmy Carter, former United Nations Ambassador Jeanne Kirkpatrick, Mexican writer Carlos Fuentes, Pulitzer Prize winning novelist Toni Morrison, former Federal Reserve Board Chairman Paul Volcker, and former Prime Minister of Ireland Garret Fitzgerald. In fairness to these star players, it should be pointed out that most could make much more money—up to $20,000 for a single speech—on the speaking circuit. Apparently, these individuals prefer the more intimate, comprehensive relationship with students offered by the classroom setting.

But the star complex now evident among colleges and universities may represent more than a marketing tool to raise an institution's profile. It may manifest a subconscious feeling that overall faculty quality is not adequate and therefore efforts must be made to lift the reputation of the whole faculty with a few superstars. But the challenge of insuring quality faculty is a long-term national problem; it will not be solved by competition for star researchers among a handful of colleges and universities or by showcasing a few big names for one night or even one semester. The problem is much more pervasive.

It begins with the fact that a shortage of candidates for the professoriate is almost certain to occur in the 1990s and continue well into the twenty-first century. It feeds on a gut feeling that the associate professor cadre, candidates for full professor in the 1990s, is somehow sub-par. It demands a renewed emphasis on the quality of teaching and learning in America's colleges and universities. And it rests on an underlying uneasiness about change, the move toward a world economy, and the demands of the twenty-first century.

These concerns are both real and perceptional and, from either perspective, they must be dealt with in the 1990s. But will there be radical or evolutionary change? The guess here is that, barring a cataclysmic shift in the world economy or order, significant evolutionary change will be pursued on many fronts, compressing change into a much shorter than normal period of time.

POTENTIAL SOLUTIONS

The 1990s will see numerous initiatives intended to bolster the nation's supply of quality faculty. These proposals will most likely be divided into federal and non-federal funding sources. Columbia University President Michael I. Sovern recommended a number of possible federal initiatives in a January 1989 *New York Times Magazine* article.[9] They included federal funding of a sufficient number of graduate fellowships to help assure a continuous flow of first-rate doctoral candidates, and full payment for federally sponsored research—including libraries, laboratories, and equipment. These proposals, Sovern suggested, would enable the federal government to strengthen graduate education in the nation's research universities, support basic research, produce more doctorates, and keep them in the universities as faculty. Another federal effort in the 1990s may provide forgivable loans/grants for doctoral candidates who pursue college and university teaching careers. Action by the universities themselves, as well as states, private foundations, and the corporate world, can make a difference in the quality of college and university faculty by the turn of the century—if it is begun now. The following are a few suggestions for action:

• Mechanisms must be found to delay the retirement of top faculty instead of structuring financial reward systems which tend to push them out. Why should an early retirement system literally push out the noted scholar mentioned at the beginning of this chapter when he could have comfortably remained in his long-standing, highly productive faculty position? For the best and most effective faculty, the idea of early retirement and buy-outs is simply crazy! These individuals represent a tremendous national resource. We must have access to the minds and experience of our top university faculty long after they are fifty-five or sixty-five or even seventy-five—they represent a tremendous resource. With these early retirement systems in place, it is unreasonable to expect senior faculty to work for little more than retirement pay. And it is more economical to encourage their continued service, with compensation for both retirement and current service, than to lose them or try to replace them quickly via crash programs. Obviously, new approaches in this area are imperative.

• It may be possible for colleges and universities to lure back some of the thousands of Ph.D.s who have left academe over the past two decades due to a temporary excess of doctorates or greener pastures elsewhere. Many of these individuals may have a desire to try teaching or to share their accumulated work and research experiences with a new generation of Americans. Colleges and universities may be able to benefit from the business sector's early retirement programs, which, like education, also launch perfectly capable people toward a second career. To nurture these transitions, educational institutions must be sensitive to differences between corporate and academic environments and ensure an appropriate adjustment period for professionals in industry and government as they acclimate to the university scene.

Several successful examples of this reverse migration back to the university can be found in Virginia. A civil engineering faculty member at Pratt Institute left to start his own company. Later, however, after his firm was bought out in a hostile takeover, this sixty—year-old businessman became dean of a business school.

A well-known electrical engineering professor at the Massachusetts Institute of Technology left MIT in 1972 for government service and later ran a major electronics corporation. In his late fifties, he discovered an itch to teach, conduct research, and complete the last two volumes of his planned five-volume series on communications engineering. In his first year with a Virginia university, this man returned to teaching to share his experiences in government and private sector service, attracted new students to the university, and raised enough money ($17 million over five years) to start a major research center.

Colleges can find it rewarding to search out many well-qualified doctorates and lure them back to campus. But they must be proactive in their efforts; those who are will certainly be rewarded.

• Universities should abolish the "serf system" for graduate students which, as it has evolved in the latter half of the twentieth century, traps young academics in poorly paid positions on the lower rungs of the academic ladder. By exploiting these young people instead of nurturing them, a generation of future faculty are being depleted in advance. Graduate assistants should be paid a fair and competitive wage; they should be cared for, mentored, and otherwise encouraged to think positively about teaching and research positions in the academy.

• Colleges and universities should begin to distinguish more clearly between teaching and research faculty, and between undergraduate and graduate faculty. All faculty cannot be treated as researchers and forced to spend countless hours writing articles for obscure journals read by few people inside or outside the academy. Teaching faculty must continue a level of scholarship to stay current, but to insist that all faculty pretend to be involved in basic research drives good teachers from the academy.

• Colleges and universities must expand on the idea of joint appointments with business and industry. Many young scientists and engineers attracted by the dynamics and compensation of the market would make good teachers and may have a desire to teach. Why not seek out such potential faculty in a true partnership with business and industry?

• New consideration must be given to working spouses. In the past, many institutions refused to consider employment for spouses, but in today's increasingly competitive environment, it is not uncommon for a college or university to recruit a couple to the faculty or at least offer career provisions for the spouse of a serious recruit.

• Other personnel policies are also currently under scrutiny, including such benefits as child care. Clearly, colleges and universities with the best and most progressive benefits packages will find themselves in a better competitive position in recruiting new quality faculty in the 1990s. In fact, progressive personnel policies may become more important than traditional considerations.

Though market forces, job opportunities, and better salaries may entice more young people into college teaching, the academy must assume more responsibility for both the quantity and quality of its professoriate. This issue cannot be taken lightly: the future of American higher education depends as much on the quality of its teachers as on anything else.

6

Institutional Ethics

In government, in business, even in religion, questions of ethics have attracted widespread public attention in recent years. We live in a complex age beset by moral confusion. With so many sides to every issue, who can say anymore what's right and what's wrong? When it comes to matters of conscience, where do we draw the line?

Higher education is not immune to this dilemma. Colleges and universities recognize that students headed for the complexities of twenty-first century life will face quandaries light-years beyond Philosophy 101. Consequently, courses in applied ethics are sprouting up in all fields, from medicine to business and international trade. Ironically, however, the same administrators promoting ethics curricula often find themselves in situations that challenge the values of their institutions. All too often, institutional integrity is diluted as administrators emulate the quixotic values present in other areas of American society.

Consider, for example, the implications of the following scenarios, which represent confusing new dilemmas, as well as established, but questionable practices in higher education. These actual incidents only begin to illustrate the many gray areas routinely confronted by college and university administrators.

THE CORPORATE QUANDARY

The two top administrators of an up-and-coming regional university sat at breakfast with "Moneybags," a well-heeled local developer. According to rumor, the former immigrant turned entrepreneur reaped hundreds of millions of dollars during the land boom of the 1980s.

As the trio sipped coffee and munched toast, "Moneybags" described his latest project, a controversial billion dollar development proposal, encompassing over 1000 undeveloped acres.

The land in question consisted of several prime private parcels, which Moneybags had reserved with an option to buy, plus a hazardous waste storage site. Before he could realize his plans for the acreage, however, Moneybags faced several hurdles; the most formidable of these was local opposition to development.

Area residents concerned about traffic and environmental problems had successfully blocked several previously proposed uses of the private land. At the same time, with support from government representatives, the citizens had waged a decade-long fight demanding closure and cleanup of the hazardous waste site.

Savvy to these concerns, Moneybags had entered the picture with a proposal to clean up the dump in exchange for title to the site, which he planned to merge with the private land in a 1,000-acre development. Further, Moneybags had maneuvered to convince area residents his new development would create hundreds of jobs and revive their dormant local economy.

The entrepreneur outlined an appealing mixed-use complex, combining commercial and residential units, complete with modern transportation facilities, two golf courses, and—the pièce de résistance—a 200-acre high-tech center operated by a consortium of two world-class universities: a renowned foreign institution and a nationally recognized private research school located nearby.

After presenting his development proposal, Moneybags began weaving another story into the breakfast conversation. It seems he had suddenly come into a "small" windfall of $1.5 million which he'd decided to give to educational enterprises. He had already made a verbal promise to endow a $1 million chair at the private research university that was to manage the proposed high-tech research center.

The purpose of this breakfast meeting, Moneybags told the administrators, was threefold: First, he wanted to explain his development plan to "two important community leaders." Second, he wanted to ask if the regional university would like to play a part in the proposed high-tech center. Finally, he wanted to offer the school $250,000 of the windfall money for an endowed professorship.

How could the two administrators object? The overall project looked good; there was an opportunity to become involved in a high-tech center with two prestigious universities; and the $250,000 seemed like manna from heaven.

Leaving his guests to ponder his proposals, Moneybags excused himself and hurried off to present his project to the editorial board of a large daily newspaper. In the resulting article, however, there was no mention of participation by the regional university. The oversight was explained soon after when a friend of one of the administrators—also a news executive present at the editorial meeting with "Moneybags"—called to confide that the developer had expressed contempt toward the regional university, complaining that it did not carry the prestige he desired.

Concerned, the administrator decided to investigate the situation. In a few phone calls, he learned that Moneybags had met months earlier with the president of the private research university named in connection with the proposed high-tech center. Apparently, the developer solicited a promise from the university to consider joining with the foreign institution in operating the high-tech center. Moneybags' appeal included the story of his unexpected windfall and his offer of the $1 million endowment to the university.

The conversation ended with a handshake and a verbal agreement that Moneybags would send a letter promising the $1 million. The university president, in turn, agreed to consider comanaging the high-tech center. In the meantime, Moneybags could mention the university's name in connection with his proposed development.

What really happened here? With the promise of a $1 million endowment, Moneybags secured the right to use the private research university's name in negotiations with the federal government and local civic associations. Even if he stretched the truth a little concerning the university's actual commitment to his project, he knew no one would complain: one million dollars was at stake.

But the local university might still object to the huge development project, particularly the infusion of next-door competition from the two universities involved in the high-tech center. To head off possible complaints, Moneybags, as an afterthought, arranged the breakfast meeting—and its enticing offers. With heightened prestige and a quarter million dollars on the line, Moneybags knew it would be difficult for the regional university to object to his billion dollar deal. In fact, he now had every reason to expect the administration's support.

Is there a question of ethics here? Should the research university president have accepted the million dollar endowment or lent his university's name to a project without faculty discussion? Was he wrong, or, at the very least, woefully naive? Without question, either of these deals taken by itself would look a lot better than the two together.

Should the regional university administrators have accepted the quarter million dollar windfall and become involved in the new high-tech center, despite the risk of perceived collusion with the developer against community wishes? Do appearances matter? Will anyone even notice?

And who could blame Moneybags? Such tactics were accepted business practices in his native country. No explicit deals had been cut; everything had transpired in polite, circumventive language.

Just where should universities draw the line in corporate connections?

STUDY NOW, PAY LATER

The computer scientist and his daughter, a high school senior in the throes of the college admissions process, sat together in the posh office of a private university's admissions counselor. They were stunned.

The counselor had just tallied the total tuition, fees, and room and board costs for the coming academic year—$17,500. She watched her visitors' eyes glaze as the "sticker shock" hit them. She'd seen that look a thousand times in recent years. It was her cue to move in quickly.

"Don't get excited," the counselor began. "Let's look at your financial aid application."

She produced the paperwork, including a set of figures. "Because you scored over 1100 on your SAT, the university will give you a $3,500 academic scholarship. And because you're in-state, the state will provide a $2,500 tuition voucher. That's $6,000 off the total, bringing the cost down to $11,500. Now, according to our calculations based on your family's finances, you qualify for an $8,000 loan guaranteed by the federal government, leaving a balance of only $3,500 for the first year."

The father and daughter exchanged glances. They both realized "the bottom line" amounted to less than the cost of a year at a state university. Maybe they could afford a private college after all.

But let's replay this scenario in a different setting. "We'll cut the price $2,500; the company will kick in a $3,500 rebate; and the bank will loan you $8,000. Only $3,500 down, and you can drive this baby home today!"

With the change of a few words, the prestigious private university begins to sound like a car dealership! Are colleges right to manipulate financial aid and pricing structures to marketing advantage? Some colleges simply raise prices because their peers do, fearing lower tuition might be read as a signal of lower quality. And what about the long-term payments? As discussed in chapters 3 and 4, the prevalence of student loans has not only driven up the cost of college, but is causing thousands of young people to graduate (or not graduate) deep in debt. Is there an ethical question in increasing costs and loans to middle-income students to help finance grants to low-income students? Are student loans a blessing or a curse?

Sandra is a twenty-three-year-old stellar graduate of the state's leading university. In high school she carried a perfect 4.0 grade point average, and she scored 1260 on the SAT. While earning a bachelor of arts degree in psychology, she maintained a 3.85 GPA. But Sandra came from an economically disadvantaged family and was forced to borrow almost the entire cost of her college education. She graduated owing $19,000 in student loans.

After college, Sandra had difficulty landing a solid job. It was nearly a year before she finally accepted a position as a counselor's assistant in a children's home. Her pay: $16,000 annually. Sandra's basic living expenses—food, a car for commuting, plus one-third of the cost of a shared townhouse, left her little more than change for other budget items.

How could Sandra pay off her student loans? She didn't have the foggiest idea—until she read a newspaper article about the growing numbers of former students defaulting on college loans.

"Why not?" Sandra thought. "Everyone else is doing it. I'll just default. I'll declare personal bankruptcy and get out of this depressing mess."

As loan volumes increase and college students graduate—or drop out—with huge debts, how *will* they pay the money back? Will they come to the same conclusion as Sandra? And, if so, will defaulting on student loans perhaps set a life pattern of reneging on personal obligations—financial or otherwise? Does this phenomenon perhaps partially explain students' obsession with fields of study that pay high starting salaries?

FACULTY FRAUD

The dean of graduate studies sat alone in his office thinking about his career. The past two years had taken their toll. He had accepted a special assignment for the university during a time of controversy and inadvertently destroyed his dream of someday becoming a university president.

But now the university had just named him to one of its most prestigious and lucrative endowed chairs. Though he was respected in professional administrative circles, the dean made no claims as an academic scholar. He knew the chair was the university's way of rewarding a good soldier. At age sixty, he could soon step down from the demands of his current position, teach just two courses and indulge his passion for golf while drawing a handsome six figure salary.

Old friends had lent their support to win him the appointment. In fact, the chair of the nominating committee was an old buddy he had recruited to the university years earlier who went on to become a department chair. Just last year—at the dean's insistence—he had received his own endowed professorship.

Over the past ten years, higher education has enjoyed a healthy increase in private donations, largely in response to "eminent scholars" campaigns designed to ensure margins of excellence by attracting brilliant minds to faculty positions. Without these increased funds, most colleges and universities could not hope to compete with business, law or medicine for the talents of these outstanding professionals. Yet, institutions stand to lose credibility—and dollars—through the all-too-common practice of rewarding longevity rather than genius.

Charles Sykes has pointed out another faculty concern in his 1989 book *Profscam*. He argues that the American professoriate is cheating the nation by pushing for ever lighter teaching loads in order to devote more time to writing research papers for journals created solely as vehicles for these otherwise unpublishable articles.[1] Again, the credibility of American colleges rests on the quality of faculty. Higher education must be proactive in addressing such charges now to avoid future repercussions.

FIGURES DON'T LIE; OR, DO THEY?

The new college president faced a dilemma. He had just stepped to the helm of a principal state university in the midwest, a good school suffering from severe image problems. A failure of leadership over the past three years had resulted in a series of embarrassments, both athletic and financial. State and national press reports had been devastating, leading ultimately to a faculty revolt, resignation of the university president, and removal of several board members.

The new administrator's immediate challenge was to turn the school's public image around, and fast. He began planning a number of initiatives designed to foster positive press reports. First, he turned to a proven tactic. During his eleven-year tenure at his previous university, he had stumbled on an idea which paid huge dividends. In fact, its success had greatly impressed the search committee and helped win him his current position. His secret? He had discovered a technique for attracting "National Merit Scholars."

The plan was simple. In the National Merit Scholarship competition, there are three levels of recognition: National Merit Semi-finalists; National Merit Finalists; and National Merit Scholars. Merit Scholars are those who actually receive scholarships from the National Merit Scholarship Corporation.

To encourage the runners-up, the corporation had recently agreed that finalists receiving a scholarship of at least $2,000 from a college or university can be designated National Merit Scholars, albeit with an asterisk by their names to distinguish between the two classes of scholarship winners.

In the early 1980s, when this practice of recruiting, then upgrading, Merit Finalists surfaced, a firestorm of accusations among institutions blazed in the national press. The primary objection raised was the public relations dimension of the issue: the institutions instigating the practice ballyhooed their resulting high enrollments of "Merit Scholars" as a sign of institutional academic quality! Most colleges and universities, however, considered the practice unbecoming and even fraudulent behavior.

But this technique had worked well for the new president before, so why not try it again? He did. After scraping together more than $100,000, he soon could boast of almost ninety "National Merit Scholars" enrolled, compared with only nineteen the year before. The university press office began touting a major turnaround under the new president. His strategy had once again proved a success.

But more problems lay ahead. The new president learned the university was losing federal research dollars. Further, in the respected National Science Foundation's ranking of schools by federal research dollars received, the university had slipped from seventy-second to eighty-third in the nation. This disturbing trend had to be turned around.

In reviewing the National Science Foundation report, the new administrator discovered research support could be reported via another category, one that included corporate and institutional contributions. With these extra dollars padding the totals, the university's rank improved measurably. Intrigued, he decided to take a closer look at this area.

Examining the university's records, the president found a carefully computed set of figures had been used to estimate research support. "Too conservative," he thought. In consultation with university accountants, he discovered that slight changes in a few assumptions (stipulating twelve hours, not eight, as a standard full teaching load, for example) could dramatically enhance the research support total from the university. Consequently, in its next reporting cycle, the National Science Foundation showed the university had jumped to forty-second in total research dollars.

Predictably, the university's public relations unit lost no time in cheering the new, improved ranking, even precipitating a statewide stir by shamelessly comparing their campus to specific other state universities. In the competition for federal research dollars, however, little had changed: the school ranked seventy-ninth.

The practice of "refiguring" institutional statistics to enhance image or gain market advantage is perhaps best illustrated by recent manipulations of Scholastic Aptitude Test (SAT) scores.

(The primary college admissions test in twenty-one states, the Scholastic Aptitude Test (SAT) is administered by the Educational Testing Service, Inc.—commonly referred to as the College Board—of Princeton, New Jersey, and is intended to assist colleges in placing students. The basic test is divided into two parts, verbal and mathematical, each scored from 200 to 800. The minimum combined score is 400; the maximum, 1600. The national average combined score hovers around 900.)

Though the College Board records each student's scores and the names of institutions receiving those scores, it does not know which school students ultimately attend. It is up to individual institutions to report average composite SAT scores for their entering classes. One result of this situation, exacerbated by a growing competition for "market share" of new students, is the increasing use—and misuse—of SAT scores as an indicator of academic quality. In the 1980s, amid fierce competition for students, SAT composites emerged as formidable ammunition in the public relations war. The 1988 *U.S. News and World Report* special issue on America's best colleges, for example, relied heavily on institutional SAT scores.

As one might guess, this emphasis on SAT averages has led to the practice of "refiguring" institutional SATs. News reports have documented the shading of SAT averages in order to publicize the highest possible institutional score.[2] Colleges and universities participating in this trend cite two theories to justify their methodology in "refiguring" average institutional SATs: First, they maintain that any student admitted as special admissions (athletes, minorities, performing artists, and children of alumni, for example) do not reflect the institution's regular admissions standards. Thus, the schools' publicized SAT averages do not include scores by students in these special categories.

The second theory appears even more dubious. It presumes that only those who enroll for the first time in the fall (less special admissions) should be included in composite SATs. If, for example, certain

high risk students are required to take courses in the summer between high school and college as a condition of admission, they are
not counted in the institutional SAT average.

The *New York Times* estimated the typical institution exempts
30–35 percent of their lower-scoring students from the school's reported average. And it gets worse! In some states, the lowest reported institutional average registers fifty points above the average
for all high school seniors taking the test. And the weighted institutional averages, both public and private, reportedly run 150 to 200
points above the state average. Unbelievably, this obvious charade
continues unchallenged; apparently, no one in any state is willing to
say the emperor has no clothes.

The practice of massaging statistics raises difficult questions of
institutional integrity. Is there any way to gain control of the escalating marketing war where higher prices, higher SATs, more National
Merit Scholars (even second class scholars), and higher rankings
have become the predominant indicators of quality? Again, perhaps
the toughest question of all is, How do such practices reflect on students and their behavior?

ATHLETIC INDISCRETIONS

Karl came from a poor but proud inner-city family. He and his sister
were reared by a grandmother who worked two jobs to support the
children. But still she made time to insure their involvement in
church and sports as well as school. Karl excelled in basketball. By
his senior year in high school, he had become a much sought-after
prospect among college scouts.

As the recruitment process unfolded, Karl was dazzled by the
limelight and the attention of well-dressed, fast-talking college basketball coaches, who also impressed him as sincere and caring. It
was difficult to choose among them, but he finally decided on a private, church-affiliated university with a strong academic reputation
and an up-and-coming basketball program. Later, however, Karl
learned that his highly prized basketball scholarship (worth $16,000
in tuition room and board) did not include spending money or transportation expenses to and from school. And so his grandmother
dipped into her savings for travel expenses, clothes, and pocket cash.

Karl arrived on campus a celebrity, expecting to take the school
to the National Collegiate Athletic Association (NCAA) tournament, a
surefire path to big money and national recognition for any college.
Though Karl's new clothes could not compare with the designer
threads of the other students, whose median family income sur-

passed $100,000 that year, anonymous donors saw that he was well-dressed. Grandmother's spending money seemed petty cash compared to the bankrolls of other students, but this posed no big problem either; handshakes often deposited $100 bills in his palm.

And at parties, when people all around him began sniffing cocaine, Karl couldn't resist. College was a whirl. His basketball prowess increased; life spun faster and faster. After two years, schoolwork and the goal of a degree had been shoved to the back of Karl's mind. But then, suddenly, his grades came crashing down, and the NCAA came investigating. In the end, Karl was declared academically ineligible to play. He left school; his coach was fired; the school was placed on athletic probation. Karl's dream had become a nightmare.

Where were the administrators of this university, and others like it where similar scenes have played out, those individuals responsible for preventing this sort of catastrophe? Another scene from the world of college athletics may shed some light on this puzzling situation.

Two university vice presidents talked quietly over lunch. One had just weathered a year-long public wrangle as his school, under the spotlight of a major NCAA investigation, attempted to force its football coach to resign.

The other vice president told of a similar situation at his school where administrators were in the process of dismissing a veteran basketball coach who, just the year before, signed a "lifetime" ten-year contract. But things had since gone sour, and now university administrators wanted him out.

Despite the wrenching nature of these delicate personnel matters, the two vice presidents expressed a shared enthusiasm. As advisors to their respective university presidents, they realized a sense of righteous accomplishment in pushing successfully to oust the tainted coaches and thus safeguard the integrity of their academic institutions.

Three years later, as college presidents, these same two men each experienced a prolonged, painful, and highly publicized basketball scandal at their schools. The NCAA investigated; the publicity mounted; and, finally, both presidents fired their coaches. But gone was the earlier sense of excitement and victory. As the final decision-maker, each discovered, the process proved extremely painful and exhausting.

But the administrators' troubles were far from over. With their basketball programs in shambles, both universities faced athletic department deficits due to decreased contributions and television revenues. Consequently, searches began on both campuses for a "name" coach to transform a battered basketball squad into a national power. In each case, no expense was spared in hiring a celebrated new head coach. As one "alum" explained, "You've got to spend money to make money."

How could two principled college officials so easily succumb to the debatable practice of paying top dollar (as much as $500,000 annually) for big-name coaches? Most observers will agree that money is a major force in the continuing American university athletic scandal, yet college and university presidents seem powerless to even stand up and protest. A few have tried, only to be criticized so harshly that they retreated into their offices, never to be heard from again on the subject.

College sports stand in a peculiar position today. Money is flowing into college athletic departments in record volumes. The typical Division 1-A football school reports an annual athletic budget of $10 million to $15 million. Revenues come from contributions, gate receipts, television contracts, NCAA post-season play, bowl appearances, athletic-related side business, and student fees. All but the most successful programs are highly dependent on student fees.

Despite this influx of dollars, no more than a half-dozen institutions (and perhaps only Notre Dame) realize a net positive cash flow from their athletic endeavors. Most colleges are either mired in debt or scrambling to keep their financial noses above water. The struggle is a continuous one, and the upward spiral of athletic costs seems out of control.

Who benefits from the dollars generated by these runaway costs? Certainly not the student! NCAA rules governing athletic scholarships barely allow coverage of tuition, fees, room and board, and books. Economically disadvantaged students often lack funds for incidental expenses (haircuts, dry cleaning, etc.), not to mention health care and transportation between school and home. Further compounding the problem, in order to cut costs many colleges have limited both the value and number of scholarships awarded.

In most cases, institutions don't benefit from athletic income either. As indicated, most colleges must impose hefty athletic fees on their students just to make operating budget ends meet. But remaining competitive requires bigger, more modern facilities involving additional capital expenditures and highly creative financing.

While student players and institutions struggle to cover basic expenses, however, some coaches—primarily basketball and football coaches—do very well. The total income package for a typical big-time basketball coach might look like this:

Salary	$80,000
Television show	25,000
Promotional use of Brand X ball	25,000
Promotional use of Brand Y shoes	50,000
Summer camp profits	100,000
Speaking	10,000
Total	**290,000**

Though the typical coach may not be adding directly to his institution's financial woes, this multisource salary structure can lead to cheating. A coach knows all too well that if his team doesn't win, he may lose his job and all its attendant perks. And where else can a thirty to forty-five-year-old with a B.S. and ten to fifteen years coaching experience make $300,000 a year? Consequently, a well-compensated coach who sees his program slipping may be tempted to cheat. Violating NCAA rules is not breaking the law. So why not slip a $1,000 bill in a basketball shoe to keep a star player happy? Who will know?

Such inequities and indiscretions are not lost on the student athletes. They see that coaches are well paid, drive a new loaner car each year, and travel extensively, while players struggle to balance studies, workouts, and games, yet sometimes can't even scrape up enough cash for a haircut. So why not pressure the assistant coach for travel money to go home? Why not ask his help in arranging automobile financing or selling complimentary tickets to a big game? Why not cheat? Everyone else is doing it, right?

What lessons are colleges and universities really teaching their students when institutional values become muddled? If colleges offer ethics courses that scrutinize practices in business and science, shouldn't they quietly examine their own actions in the same objective light? Why haven't faculty said "stop?" Why haven't the national associations taken up the ethics issue? Where are the American Association of University Professors? Where is the United States Department of Education? Where are the accrediting agencies? Who will provide the uncompromising leadership so critically needed in higher education today?

A PROPOSAL: ETHICS AND VALUES IN HIGHER EDUCATION

Unlike many segments of American society, colleges and universities are not monitored by a regulatory body. There is no cousin of the securities and exchange commission to confront the equivalent of "insider trading" in American higher education. In fact, there is not even a professional code of ethics governing American colleges and universities.

Without self-regulation, questionable issues such as those discussed in this chapter may bring the strong hand of Congress to bear on American institutions of higher education. Already, congressional hearings have focused on intercollegiate athletics and the national demand for affordable higher education. In addition, national lawmakers have investigated the need for heightened federal action against institutions with high student loan default rates, and they've questioned peer review as a sufficient control mechanism in monitoring university research efforts.

Indeed, American higher education seems to be careening toward a crisis in institutional integrity and an unfriendly takeover by government. But this unpleasant denouement can be avoided if the academy takes charge of its destiny and disciplines itself. Two steps are required:

1. Accrediting agencies must stop counting library books and tallying faculty workloads, and instead pay more attention to the ethics, values, and integrity of institutions. Regular accrediting bodies should make integrity their primary standard.

2. National associations must develop a code of ethics, including enforcement provisions, for their members. Associations should stand for something other than special interest issues.

In conclusion, colleges and universities, like all American institutions, from business to government to religion, display symptoms of the ubiquitous greed of the 1980s. Clearly, something must change. The question is, Will the requisite change result from catastrophe or from leadership? Only time will tell.

7

Science, Technology, and Economic Competitiveness

The coupling of American education with the nation's performance in the global marketplace has drawn increasing consideration in recent years. Especially since the 1983 release of "A Nation at Risk," United States Secretary of Education Terrel Bell's alarming report on America's education system, politicians have begun to view education as an important tool in economic development and national competitiveness.

But the link between education and national productivity can be traced back more than seven decades, to the publication of Einstein's theory of relativity in 1916. Einstein's remarkable notion seeded a fifty-year scientific revolution that ultimately resulted in a knowledge-based, integrated global economy.

ECONOMIC EVOLUTION AND EDUCATION REFORM

During the 1940s, World War II served as a catalyst in greatly accelerating the scientific revolution begun by Einstein. The America that emerged from war in 1945 had split the atom and developed major research universities underwritten by federal research and development funds. Further, the capture and importation of German rocket scientists during the war capped a fifteen-year influx into the United States of Europe's best scientific minds.

In 1957, however, America's scientific community suffered embarrassment when the Russians, with the help of their captured German scientists, launched Sputnik, the first man-made Earth satellite. But Sputnik's historic flight launched the Cold War space race, and the resulting generation of telecommunications satellites launched the current information age.

The year 1970 marked the one-hundredth anniversary of the flowering of the Industrial Revolution and the ensuing reformation of higher education. But the 1970 OPEC oil boycott precipitated a fuel crisis that turned the world's economy upside down, tipping the scales decidedly away from industrial dominance and toward a science-driven, knowledge-based global economy. By the mid–1980s, economists stood baffled by the economic repercussions of America's continuing shift into the Information Age. In spite of large budget and import deficits, the United States enjoyed a strong, if uneven, economy.

With this conversion from an industrial to information-based economy, business leaders and politicians, particularly governors, began to view education as the key to twenty-first century economic competitiveness at all levels—local, state, national, and international. In September 1989, President George Bush expressed federal concern over America's education system by calling the nation's governors together in Charlottesville, Virginia for a national summit on education. Bush, who early in his term proclaimed himself an "education president," seemed bent on rallying an education-conscious team of governors in an unprecedented way. Signals from the summit confirmed that both the president and the governors believed quality education holds the key to the nation's competitive participation in the world economy of the twenty-first century.

Bush's national summit reinforced a tide of corrective action by politicians and educators initiated in 1983 by Terrel Bell's grim conclusion: "If a foreign power tried to impose this education system on the U.S. we would go to war." Since the publication of "A Nation at Risk," practically every state has launched a high profile reform effort. Public school curricula have been upgraded; teacher preparation guidelines have been altered. Electives such as art, music, vocational subjects, and special interest courses are being eliminated in favor of more "academic" subjects. Many schools have adopted "no pass, no play" rules for student athletes. Talk continues regarding school choice (options beyond the neighborhood school), longer school days, and a longer academic year. Mindful of the new global economy, governors are pushing for more foreign language instruction, even though most people who have studied a foreign tongue are unable to read a menu in that language.

At the college and university level, too, talk of the relationship between higher education and economic development has accelerated since the early 1980s. Even political leaders who once discounted high-tech as hype have changed their minds. The idea that America's competitive strength and economic future hinge on the quality of her work force, including those individuals involved in research and development, has now gained seemingly irrefutable relevance. This recognition has led to a plethora of new state policies, programs and initiatives designed to foster a productive symbiosis between higher education and higher productivity.

The links between national competitiveness and education have been discussed at length in other volumes; the shortcomings of American education as measured against other countries and our own past are also well documented. Rather than attempt, then, to reiterate these arguments, this chapter will focus on the following selected topics: student interest in science and mathematics; illiteracy and a competitive work force; new approaches to transferring technology from the laboratory to the production line; business and industry involvement in education; and technology, education, and the twenty-first century.

STUDENT INTEREST IN SCIENCE AND MATHEMATICS

A nineteen-year-old economics major visited his faculty advisor. His request? To redirect his program of study toward a bachelor of arts rather than a bachelor of science degree.

"Wait a minute!" the advisor cautioned. "If you change you'll need two years of a foreign language."

"Yes," the student agreed, "but that's better than taking more math."

"But you already have one semester of calculus; you only need a second semester of calculus and one statistics course," the professor said.

"Yes, I know," the student said, "but I've decided to do it."

This intimidated economics student illustrates the mindset of many American young people toward science and mathematics. For some reason these subjects pose a mystery to many Americans, especially students facing calculus and chemistry exams. This phobia raises particular concerns considering today's young people are entering high school just one generation after a national emphasis on science education that followed the Soviet Union's launch of Sputnik in 1957. Even more alarming, scientific literacy will become increasingly critical in the science-driven, knowledge-based economy of the twenty-first century. Today's students must understand math and science in order to function in tomorrow's workplace.

Even though state requirements for high school graduation now include more science and math, few students emerge from high school with a firm grasp of these subjects. Part of the reason for this deficiency can be attributed to a dilution of traditional science and math curricula by public school systems struggling to meet expanded state requirements. To accommodate an increased number of science and math students, for example, many high schools now offer three levels of chemistry: conceptual chemistry, chemistry, and advanced placement chemistry.

Consequently, though unprecedented numbers of high school students are studying chemistry, only the top, college-bound students receive the benefits of advanced placement chemistry, while a large percentage of students mark time in conceptual or non-math chemistry courses.

How can Americans hope to compete successfully in a global market if high school students learn chemistry on a non-math basis and college students prefer four semesters of language to only one semester of calculus?

There must be a better way. Let us look at the calculus question in particular. While unquestionably perplexing at first, calculus is in reality easy to understand and eminently practical. In fact, the practicality of calculus can answer those age-old questions of students: "Why do I need to know this?" "How will I ever use this?" Calculus should therefore be integrated into the study of mathematics at the earliest possible moment. It should be the key to understanding not only the potential, but the excitement of mathematics.

Yet, students at all levels are afraid even to attempt advanced mathematics. And no wonder. Most American universities now teach calculus in large sections of sixty to ninety students. Often these classes are conducted by graduate assistants and part-time faculty members, many of whom are foreign nationals with limited English skills, a complication that only adds to the math mystique. At one university, students demanded that graduate teaching assistants be required to take an English language proficiency test; over half failed.

On the other hand, calculus is a subject that can benefit from cost-effective, technological teaching innovations. Why not make it a bonafide university course—taught by the best senior faculty in math, science, engineering and business, and augmented by television, computers, laboratories, and tutorials? The crucial importance of science and mathematics in a technological society merits such extraordinary efforts by colleges and universities to excite students of these fundamental and fascinating subjects.

ILLITERACY AND A COMPETITIVE WORK FORCE

Who hasn't seen the story on television? A thirty-year-old father has just learned to read, and it has saved his job. He was a high school dropout with mild learning disabilities, but had never told even his wife and children that he could not read. Instead, he had learned to cope in an increasingly complex world. But recently his job had become more technical; it required reading now, and he could no longer fake it. He was in danger of losing his economic independence when chance drew him into a literacy development program at the local community college.

This story and others like it are often told in public service advertisements on television. Documentaries and newspaper articles also attest to the serious problem of illiteracy in America. In addition, First Lady Barbara Bush has emerged as a national leader calling for solutions to the dilemma. And in the state of Virginia, Jeanne Baliles, wife of a former governor, launched the Virginia Literacy Foundation to help eliminate illiteracy in that state.

The problem of illiteracy in contemporary America is widely recognized by leaders in education, politics, and industry. In the workplace, the spread of technology, necessary to support the nation's knowledge-based economy, continues to increase the basic skill levels required for employment. At the same time, an expansion of the economy, coupled with a decline in the number of eighteen-year-olds available to enter the work force, has contributed to widespread skilled labor shortages. American industry needs more skilled, literate workers. And while the impact of illiteracy on the work force raises concerns for business, industry, and governmental services, it exacts a more humiliating toll on the affected worker.

What to do about the problem of illiteracy in America remains an open question. However, several approaches are emerging:

• Most education experts see public schools as the best place to attack illiteracy—early enough to avoid remedial programs later. Much effort is currently being directed toward emphasizing reading skills in the primary grades and in state-sponsored early education programs modeled after Head Start (the successful federal preschool program), which accept children as young as four. The outcome of such programs remains dubious, however. If children are not learning to read in traditional first-grade programs, educators cannot expect a magic response to the same type of program just because it is introduced two years earlier. Many experts are now convinced that a major revamping of the schools is necessary to attack illiteracy and other nagging education problems.

• Businesses should and are doing more to mitigate the problem of illiteracy. Many firms now conduct literacy classes in their own facilities, on their own time, and at their own expense. American business and industry cannot wait for long-term solutions; they need literate workers now, and it is cost-effective for them to actively pursue their own solutions to the problem.

• Community colleges have long been involved in remedial education and have recently moved into a leadership role in the national effort to combat illiteracy. Southeast Community College in Lincoln, Nebraska, for example, has attracted national recognition for its partnership with area industries in literacy training. [1]Community colleges nationwide are adding literacy training as an additional function of their educational mission.

• Finally, it is important to note that public school districts across the nation have long offered basic adult education and are expanding those services. Federal funds for such adult educational programs were increased by some 60 percent between fiscal 1986 and 1989.[2]

Illiteracy presents a long-term, mammoth problem for the United States. This nation is home to millions of adult illiterates, and each year their numbers grow by hundreds of thousands. Illiteracy must be attacked simultaneously from both ends and in the middle—before school, during the early grades, and in the adult population. Schools, community colleges, business, and industry must join forces in collaboration with civic and nonprofit groups to safeguard America's competitive spirit by ending the national blight of illiteracy.

NEW METHODS OF TRANSFERRING TECHNOLOGY FROM THE LABORATORY TO THE PRODUCTION LINE

Once state government leaders discovered high technology and its reported potential for economic development, ideas for exploiting this lucrative new trend emerged and spread across the nation. Early in the high-tech movement, many governors and other state leaders recognized that two significant technological and economic centers, California's Silicon Valley and Boston's Route 128 corridor, were largely stimulated by major higher education concentrations. In California, Stanford and other institutions in the San Jose area spurred the development of Silicon Valley; in Massachusetts, Harvard, MIT, and some sixty other colleges and universities contributed to the growth of Route 128's high-tech community.

Surmising that higher education held the key to modern economic development, leaders in almost every state launched at least a minor effort to encourage a marriage between state research colleges and high-tech development. Some states, including Maryland, completely reorganized their systems of higher education to foster the growth of a thriving high-tech economy.

But many states—not willing to reorganize their public colleges and universities or, for political reasons, to distinguish between them by favoring certain campuses with high-tech centers—established new agencies, organizations, or foundations to promote high-tech development. These organizations offered incentives for university/industry collaboration in research, created high-tech centers of excellence, and invented new schemes for transferring technology through the university to business and industries. In addition, these organizations spawned many small business development centers, international trade centers, and industrial incubator facilities.

The best examples of such state high-tech initiatives can be found in Ohio's Thomas Edison Foundation and Pennsylvania's Ben Franklin Partnership. These organizations have proven to be cost-effective avenues for promoting university/industry collaboration and for building university research capabilities. Texas and a few other states where high-tech development efforts focus on institutions have also achieved significant success in wedding higher education with modern industry.

On the whole, technology foundations and similar state initiatives have enjoyed modest to limited success, although little state funding has been invested. But in Virginia, the state's Center for Innovative Technology remains troubled despite construction of a major facility ($40 million), the leadership of four presidents (at $100,000 per year) and expenditures totalling some $100,000,000. By contrast, the most successful state-sponsored efforts to link higher education with high-tech development have been characterized by a modest start, good leadership, and a solid program built gradually over the years.

At least one state has experimented with hiring technology transfer agents in community colleges as another means of linking higher education with industry. While successful in providing services and general information to businesses, however, these agents have failed in effectively transferring university technology to businesses due to a lack of university interest.

It is puzzling that few states have attempted to use the existing state extension services of land grant universities as conduits for transferring high technology from the laboratory to the workplace. This nation's cooperative extension service provides the world's best example of successfully applying university research to agricultural or industrial use. Why haven't the states utilized the extension service more effectively in transferring fresh technology to American industry?

BUSINESS AND INDUSTRY INVOLVEMENT IN EDUCATION

The American business community has known for a long time (at least since a 1948 study by the United States Chamber of Commerce) that quality education is synonymous with higher levels of business activity. In recent years, feeling the sting of aggressive worldwide competition, American business leaders have learned firsthand that skilled, educated employees will be the essential ingredient of a strong twenty-first century economy. Consequently, despite education's traditional fear of corporate influence, the nation's companies have developed a remarkable interest in the quality and potential of American education.

Realizing that today's economy requires ever higher levels of technical and thinking skills, the business community has become a great supporter and challenger of American education. Not only is industry collaborating with colleges and universities on research and business development, but corporate America is also providing involved leadership across a broad range of educational issues and initiatives. In Fairfax County, Virginia, for example, business leadership has formed the Fairfax Schools Educational Foundation to stimulate interaction between the area's schools and corporate community. Various community businesses participate in an Adopt-a-School-Program—an early identification program designed to stimulate minority enrollments in area colleges—and sponsor laboratories in the county's new Thomas Jefferson High School for Science and Technology.

Public colleges and universities are also enjoying increased corporate support, indicative of an extraordinary recent development in American life. Just two decades ago, public institutions conducted few capital campaigns, but today successful $100 million campaigns are commonplace. And modern corporate support encompasses much more than departments of engineering, business, and other disciplines promising direct payoffs to the business community. Concert halls, minority scholarships, plus a wide variety of projects that advance or create a margin of excellence, are now often funded from corporate contributions.

The American business community of the 1990s is led by better-educated, more open-minded leaders than in the past. Not only are these modern business titans promoting education for their employees and their children, but they are also willing to involve themselves personally for the good of the larger community and overall quality of life. This new attitude provides a resource for educators to maximize, while leaving behind education's past suspicions of corporate involvement.

TECHNOLOGY, EDUCATION, AND THE TWENTY-FIRST CENTURY

Without question, the world of the 1990s shows the influence of technological revolution. Computer chips and communications satellites have profoundly changed the way people in developed countries live and work. For some reason, however, technology has not been fully utilized to dramatically improve learning.

To be sure, personal computers have permeated the educational system, from elementary school classrooms to post-doctoral research labs. Growing progressively less expensive and more user-friendly with each new product generation, these machines have transformed administrative operations and faculty duties. In addition, computer networking is a burgeoning phenomenon both on campus and in society at large; teleconferencing is steadily dropping in cost; and interactive television is increasing in usage. But replacing the teacher with technology, either as a self-learning tool or to increase an instructor's effectiveness, remains an elusive goal. Why isn't technology more directly influencing teaching and learning?

A possible explanation is the broad scale of instructional needs, requiring affordable technology for mass use. But affordability comes only in the second or third stage of technological development. Early personal computers, for example, were often difficult to operate, and they cost eight to ten times their price today, less than a decade later. Because of this affordability factor, budget-conscious educational institutions find it extremely difficult to remain on the cutting edge of technology. Once technological advances become affordable enough for mass use, they are quickly eclipsed by new state-of-the-art designs. Illustrating this problem is the story of a university president who, in the 1950s, became sold on the idea of educational television's revolutionizing college instruction; he ordered a television set for every classroom. The next year, color televisions appeared on the market.

Though technology can be useful in education and even enhance instruction in some cases, it may play a greater role in changing the system. The current structure of American higher education reflects the industrial age. Credit hours, grade levels, graduate school, teaching formats, departments, and hierarchy all reflect the assembly line mentality of a bygone age. Students are processed, sequenced, and standardized with pre-testing and post-testing to insure quality control.

The current organization of educational institutions, from grade schools to universities, could well be the Achilles heel where educational reform is most needed and, consequently, where technology could wield the greatest impact. In the grade schools, for example, the one-room school is often exalted as a model learning environment. But the small neighborhood school was abandoned long ago in favor of mass, extended public schooling. An industrial society's drive for efficient use of resources (such as libraries) led to consolidated schools, school districts, and a massive hierarchy. The resulting bureaucracy keeps on growing, while commitment to teaching, the sole concern of the one-room school, shrinks proportionately. Ten years ago the typical suburban school district spent 60 percent of its resources on teachers' salaries; in 1988 that average had dropped to 40 percent.[3]

If technology could be used to reduce this administrative "blob" (former United States Secretary of Education William Bennett's description) while at the same time recapture some of the best elements of the one-room school, education would have achieved a major advancement. If, for example, within existing physical facilities, schools could be reorganized into systems of small schools (100 or so pupils) staffed by five or six teachers working as a team, united, supported, and empowered by technology, a radical improvement in the education of Americans could result.

In higher education, colleges and universities are faced with the dual challenge of first building critical mass in the form of faculty, programs, and facilities, and then distributing educational services to users. In hyper-growth areas around the country, regional universities are expected to build mass and distribute services simultaneously. But how does a university meet the complex needs of a new metropolitan configuration characterized by networks of far-flung urban villages—all demanding excellence in higher education? Higher education's response to the challenge of effectively massing and distributing limited resources—whether in teaching calculus or serving a complex of urban communities—must include a commitment to the fullest possible exercise of modern technology.

RESEARCH AND ECONOMIC DEVELOPMENT

When American Telephone & Telegraph broke up under a federal antitrust mandate on January 1, 1984, admirers of the company's deep commitment to research wondered about the fate of AT&T Bell Laboratories—the great American invention factory. The transistor, the laser, the solar cell, sound motion pictures, the communications satellite, the science of radio astronomy, and crucial evidence supporting the "Big Bang" theory—all these discoveries originated at Bell Labs. Without the vast revenue base provided by AT&T's operating companies, would Bell Labs—for most of its sixty-two years, the premier corporate research facility in the United States—wither into just another run-of-the-mill industrial R & D operation?

Bell Labs survived the AT&T break-up and continues to prosper. Not only did basic research operations emerge largely unscathed, but Bell Labs is also now branching into new commercial endeavors, including venture R & D firms and participation in other industries as far afield from telecommunications as airlines and shipping.

American colleges and universities can learn much from the world's premier research institution—primarily, that basic and applied research are compatible. Over the years of Bell Labs' operation, basic research has consistently absorbed about 10 percent of manpower and spending, while applied research consumes 90 percent of the budget.

At a 1989 meeting of 1,400 college and university administrators, Harvard president Derek Bok suggested that American institutions of higher education should imitate this emphasis on research applications.

"Institutions can't go on enjoying the benefits of taxpayer support, and being the celebrated centers of respected learning and discovery," Bok said, "unless we are prepared to use those abilities in some substantial part to help the society that sustains us."[4]

The success of Bell Labs, plus the advice of Bok and a growing number of others, suggests a major challenge for American higher education in the 1990s: finding practical uses for research. Applying laboratory technology to industry will have direct and positive results on this nation's ability to compete successfully in a global marketplace.

University research efforts have played this catalytic role before. Research in American universities can be traced to the proactive establishment of Johns Hopkins University and Hospital in 1867. Building upon that beginning, a series of land grant acts—the 1862 Morrill Act, the 1887 Hatch Act, and the 1914 Smith-Lever Act—furnished the basis of the modern land grant university. The work of

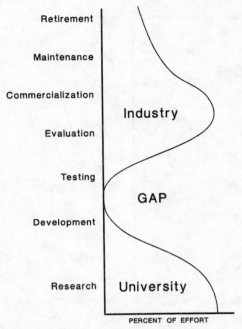

FIGURE 7.1. Life Cycle of a Product

these institutions, through their experiment stations and state cooperative extension services, provides one of the world's best examples of technology and higher education working together. Research by America's land grant institutions enabled this nation to become a world leader in food production.

Yet a rule of thumb in agriculture is that it takes ten years to fully integrate a laboratory discovery into the production cycle. This challenge of transferring technology from the laboratory to the production line continues, becoming ever more critical as technology speeds the rate of new advancements. Figure 7.1 illustrates the challenge.

In addition to a time lag between the lab and the production line, research application is often further delayed by development and testing procedures. Consequently, many good ideas lie dormant or succumb to stillbirth as newer concepts beat them to the marketplace. Much talk about new technology transfer initiatives has focused on this failure. In an effort to bridge the testing gap and expedite research application, institutions such as the Ben Franklin Partnership in Pennsylvania have been designed to promote university and industry collaboration in research as shown in figure 7.2.

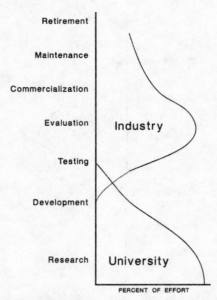

FIGURE 7.2. Life Cycle of a Product, with Technology Transfer

Whatever good may come of these efforts, Derek Bok's challenge to American higher education to focus more on practical applications of university research bears serious consideration in this age of technology. What university, like Bell Laboratories, can claim its research efforts are split 90/10, applied vs. basic? And yet what university can match Bell Labs' impeccable record as a research institution?

INTERNATIONALIZING HIGHER EDUCATION

Clearly, the world of the 1990s is shrinking. Jet aircraft, fax machines, computers, and satellites have transformed a diverse planet into a global community. People once separated by miles and customs can now relate, work, and socialize together.

Along with this scientific revolution, an integrated world economy has evolved, resulting in the loss of American manufacturing jobs. Under pressure from aggressive competitors in a global marketplace, the very essence of the once-dominant American economy is changing, threatening this nation's role in the world and the quality of life at home.

Americans have traditionally relied upon higher education to help sustain the nation's economy and quality of life. In a global society, clearly this role requires colleges and universities to prepare the next generation for the challenges of working and competing with people from other nations and cultures.

American colleges have thus far met this new task with a variety of responses and programs. Many institutions have renewed a foreign language requirement for admissions, while growing participation in international study programs reflects an increased student interest in other nations, particularly European countries. In 1989, this nation's first European Study Center was established at Virginia's George Mason University in anticipation of the establishment of the European Community in 1992.

Japanese/Pacific Rim study centers have proliferated at American colleges and universities during the past decade. In addition, many college presidents have explored Taiwan, Korea, China, and Japan via free junkets offered by Asian governments eager to enhance their images among influential Americans. Higher education has also continued a long-standing role in Third World countries. This involvement, often facilitated by the United States Agency for International Development, focuses on the operational/faculty level as American educators share information on health, education, and food production.

Though indicative of commendable interest in global affairs, these varied efforts at internationalizing American higher education fall short of meeting the demands imposed by a global economic community. United States colleges and universities interested in expanding their cultural vision cannot focus exclusively on European ties or substitute foreign public relations ploys for genuine cross-cultural interaction. Instead, American institutions should invest their own resources in a systematic effort to develop comprehensive, balanced international programs.

From abroad, foreign cultures are striving to strengthen ties with the United States. American institutions of higher education enjoy high regard around the world and continue to attract more and more international students.

In another recent development, foreign interests have begun purchasing American colleges. Japanese investors recently bought Colorado's Regis College; the same group is planning to open a new form college in Loudon County, Virginia, thirty-five miles west of the nation's capital. Another Japanese group has announced plans to establish a two-year college in Anne Arundel County, Maryland. And in West Virginia, a Japanese university has acquired Salem College and announced their intentions to convert the school into an American-

Japanese institution. To be governed predominantly by Japanese and operated predominantly by Americans, the new Salem-Teiko College will be restaffed to serve a student body of 500–1,000 Japanese and 500 American students.

Clearly, in higher education as in business, the Japanese are pro-active and move ahead aggressively. Are American colleges doing as much to prepare students for the twenty-first century? Should we be establishing universities in Japan? Or elsewhere? Where are the bold, proactive American initiatives that will successfully usher this nation into the new global community?

SUMMARY

The role of higher education in national competitiveness was dis-tilled in the opening paragraph of a lengthy report generated by a 1986 national conference on higher education and economic develop-ment. It read:

> "Higher education institutions in the United States constitute the single most significant resource that can influence economic development. They provide education and training that expands our human capital. They conduct basic and applied research that generate new technolo-gies, new products and new services. And they share the knowledge, re-sources and the expertise that help transfer innovations from sector to sector and help give American business a competitive edge."[5]

As the nation's primary arsenal in worldwide economic competi-tion, America's colleges and universities face a formidable challenge. Higher education must continually cross and recross the boundaries between the ivory tower and the world of work, proving itself a full partner in bringing competitive new products to market. Colleges and universities must also excite young people about science and math, tackle the growing problem of illiteracy, and ensure that com-ing generations of Americans are capable of living and working in a multicultural global society.

In short, the ivory tower must not crumble, but gather new strength as the new era of information and knowledge gains domi-nance and education becomes a way of life for America's most pro-ductive citizens. For good or ill, the future of American higher education will remain intertwined with the emerging global econ-omy. To fulfill their role in maintaining and enhancing this nation's economic competitiveness, American colleges and universities must commit themselves to meeting the unprecedented challenges of the twenty-first century.

8

The Community College Perspective

GEORGE B. VAUGHAN

In most instances, the community college perspective differs from that of the rest of higher education in degree rather than kind. Just because community college leaders are not directly concerned with the ethical issues emanating from big-time sports, for example, does not mean they are any less tempted to engage in unethical behavior than their four-year counterparts. My intent, therefore, is not to re-hash the issues discussed in chapters two through seven, but rather, to place those issues within the perspective of the community college mission.

The focal point of this discussion will be minority participation in higher education and its relationship to quality programs, financing, faculty vitality, institutional ethics, and national competitiveness. Those who have followed higher education and national demographics over the past decade should not be surprised to find that governors, college and university presidents, and other higher education professionals rank minority participation as one of the top issues facing higher education now and in the future. If the same survey were given to public school superintendents and business leaders, it is likely that minority participation in education (at all levels) would rank near the top of their priority lists also.

Minority participation in higher education has attracted state and national attention since at least 1954. But a number of factors, including the increased numbers of minorities in society, have given the issue a new twist, one that challenges America's free enterprise system as well as its social consciousness. In the 1960s and 1970s, the right of African Americans to move up the socioeconomic ladder was viewed as an ethical issue closely tied to the nation's commitment to democracy. Now, however, the issue goes beyond social consciousness, cutting to the quick of what many consider to be the main issue facing the nation—the relative competitiveness of the United States economy in the world. In the same vein, at least one scholar has concluded that public schools are not serving as avenues for Hispanics, America's fastest growing minority group, to enter the mainstream of American society. This situation exists in spite of the fact that the percentage of Hispanic students more than doubled (to almost 10 percent of the total public school population) between 1968 and 1987.

Stated another way, though in earlier decades minority participation in the mainstream of American society was predominantly a social issue, today, while still a social concern, it is predominantly an economic issue. Without an educated populace, America cannot compete in the world market—or even in the most isolated hamlet with its Wal-Mart brimming with goods from abroad. If this nation is to utilize the many talents of its diverse minority population, the higher education community, particularly community colleges with their large minority enrollments, must provide avenues for minorities to achieve their potential.

ENTER THE COMMUNITY COLLEGE

Minorities have entered community colleges in record numbers. Today, community colleges enroll 43 percent of all African Americans who attend the nation's institutions of higher education; 55 percent of all Hispanics, 41 percent of all Asians, and 57 percent of all Native Americans attend community colleges. In 1986, minorities made up 22 percent of students enrolled at community colleges. On many urban community college campuses, English as a second language ranks among the most popular courses on campus; classes are filled to capacity. Miami-Dade Community college enrolls more international students—4,730 in 1985—than any other institution of higher education in the nation (the University of Southern California ranked second with 3,761 students). Most of these students are Hispanic and require work in basic English.[1] But the community college perspective on minority enrollment involves more than numbers. How community colleges serve minorities may well determine the future usefulness of these institutions.

The community college is, first and foremost, an educational institution that to succeed must ultimately deal with social and economic issues through the educational process. Community college faculty are reminded daily that many of their students, especially minorities, come from the lower socioeconomic groups and rank at the bottom of the scale on standardized tests such as the SAT and ACT. Those who graduated from high school often ranked in the lower one-half of their graduating class. (Not all community college students are high school graduates. Others hold a GED, which does not carry high school rank, rather than a traditional high school diploma.) In essence, while community college leaders must remember that their mission is educational, they must also remember that the results of numerous social and economic problems are embodied in many of their students.

MINORITIES ON THE COMMUNITY COLLEGE CAMPUS

The educational mission of the community college, in addition to serving students who may be ill-prepared for college-level work, is to meet the nation's growing need for highly skilled technical workers at the associate's degree level. These workers include nurses and other health care associates, computer technicians, airplane mechanics, and any number of highly specialized individuals who occupy that increasingly important segment of the labor force requiring education beyond high school but below the bachelor's degree level.

The community college thus faces conflicting sets of expectations while trying to fulfill higher education's traditional mission, which demands enrolling only those students who are "college material" (as determined by standardized tests and high school rank) and views college as culminating in the bachelor's degree.

As admirable as it may be for the community college to take on the task of educating academically weak students in highly technical fields, those institutions that limit opportunities for minorities to two-year terminal programs have failed to serve these individuals adequately and therefore have failed society. Why? In today's society, as has been true since at least the end of World War II, the stepping stone to the professions and to most positions of leadership is the bachelor's degree. The community college that fails to understand the need for a strong college transfer program fails to comprehend the needs of the nation and the role minorities must play in its future. Indeed, community colleges that limit minority participation in higher education to programs below the traditional bachelor's degree (in contrast to the now popular bachelor's of technology degree) have closed the door of opportunity for many minorities and proved correct the critics who claim that these colleges track students into dead-end jobs. The nation simply cannot afford to limit those minorities for whom the community college offers the only avenue of upward mobility.

A word of caution: Community colleges that enroll students with academic deficiencies, many of whom are minorities, must work to eradicate those shortcomings as effectively and efficiently as possible. The cliché, "the community college's open door must not become a revolving door," is especially true today when so many minority students turn to the community college in hopes of a better tomorrow. In addition to English-as-a-second-language programs, academically deficient students require more tutoring, more counseling, more individual instruction, and more encouragement than students who have, from the sixth grade or earlier, followed the academic pathway leading to the bachelor's degree and beyond.

FINANCING HIGHER EDUCATION

As suggested in chapter 3, funding higher education presents a major problem, one that, like death and taxes, is likely to be around for time eternal. Community colleges are especially strapped when it comes to funding, since most state legislatures, which grant community colleges the majority of their revenue, fund community college students at a much lower rate than students of four-year institutions. In California, for example, member institutions of the University of California system receive over $14,000 for each full-time student, whereas California community colleges (with over one million students enrolled in credit courses) receive approximately $3,000 per full-time student.[2] While funding gaps are not usually this wide, in most states community colleges suffer, not only in comparison with the rest of higher education, but also in comparison with the public schools. Further hindering the community college in its efforts to provide quality education is a scarcity of private funds (on many campuses private funds simply do not exist in significant amounts), research funds, and other sources of funding that often provide an institution with an edge of excellence. And although community colleges enroll over 40 percent of all students taking credit courses in higher education, their students received only 18.7 percent of the Pell Grants in 1986–87.[3]

In many respects, the community college has taken on one of the most difficult tasks in higher education: to educate students with special needs, many of whom are first-generation college students, come from the lower socioeconomic groups, and score in the bottom

50 percent on standardized tests. Can community colleges offer these students a quality education with minimum funding? If not, where does this leave a nation increasingly reliant upon minority workers, many of whom must be educated by the community college?

Ironically, the trend toward some colleges and universities pricing themselves out of the educational market for students with average or below average financial sources should play into the hands of community colleges, at least as far as enrolling students in the short term is concerned. One community college leader predicted in 1984 that rising costs at four-year institutions would force more strong students from middle- and low-income families into community colleges, thereby decreasing enrollments at four-year institutions, especially select private schools. While, on the surface, community colleges would appear to be winners in this scenario, there is a danger that poorly prepared students, especially minority students with little experience negotiating the higher education system, could be squeezed out of the scene completely to make room for middle-income students who cannot afford the costs of attending a four-year institution.[4] Although this prediction has not yet come true, the thesis has not been fully tested as it will be in the 1990s if costs continue to rise. Already, Virginia Governor Douglas Wilder, the nation's first elected black governor, has forbidden Virginia's community colleges to make up revenue deficiencies through tuition increases. Wilder's action stemmed from his concern that community colleges may squeeze out members of the lower socioeconomic groups.

Can community colleges cultivate alternative funding sources, as suggested in chapter 3? It is unlikely: The alumni of community colleges either go on to four-year institutions and contribute to them, or remain in relatively low-paying positions and contribute little to their institutions. In addition, most community colleges are new to fund-raising, and their inexperience places them at a decided disadvantage relative to their more experienced four-year counterparts. With few graduates in state legislatures, community colleges often get short shrift in political showdowns, thus losing potential funding. Finally, given a choice, many donors choose to support a renowned state university or private institution over the local community college.

The much-vaunted "business-industry partnership" has helped some community colleges obtain equipment and funds. But some California colleges still train airplane mechanics on World War II-type aircraft because jet engines sell for $4 million each. The most important fiscal step community college leaders have taken in the last three decades has been to establish their colleges as integral parts of the educational systems of states. This move has assured continued funding, albeit at a relatively low level in relationship to other institutions of higher education and to many public schools. The challenge now is for community college leaders to capitalize on their position within the educational and economic strata, to demonstrate their value in training that large group of technical workers who daily are becoming more crucial to the nation's economy, but who are not being trained by four-year institutions or high schools. In addition, community college leaders must demonstrate their commitment and success in working with minorities, especially by providing them with an avenue (and the requisite support) leading to the bachelor's degree. To capitalize on their current and potential contributions, community colleges must communicate their mission more effectively to national and state legislators, to local political leaders (especially in those states where community colleges receive substantial support from local taxes), to leaders of business and industry, and to the public at large.

How are community colleges doing in regard to broadening the understanding of their mission? Some progress has been made in communicating the community college's role. A recent article in the *Chronicle of Higher Education*, while entitled "Tight Funds Thwarting State's Desire to Raise 2-Year-College Quality," nevertheless noted that:

> Until recently, they [state legislators] have paid little attention to community colleges. But their interest has been rekindled [in fact, kindled for the first time] by new concerns about increasing literacy rates, improving job training, and attracting more minority students to higher reeducation—areas in which community colleges have taken the lead. In turn, those concerns have led to discussions about the quality of academic programs and the level of state financial support.[5]

Part of this communication process must be to outline clearly the role community colleges play in the total scheme of things—an essential role if minorities are to receive the education they need and deserve, and if the nation is to regain its edge in international competition and provide for the welfare of all its citizens. Without public understanding of its mission, the community college will continue to receive inadequate funding, the quality of its programs will suffer, and its students will be denied equal opportunity for quality higher education.

MAINTAINING A QUALITY FACULTY

As suggested in chapter 5, the 1990s and beyond will see a dearth of qualified faculty in all segments of higher education. Secretary of

Education Lauro Cavazos estimates that between 1995 and 2010, colleges and universities will need over 300,000 new faculty in all disciplines. Cavazos believes that the coming faculty shortage, though serious, will provide a "marvelous window of opportunity for women, Hispanics, blacks, and other minorities" to enter the faculty pool.[6]

Can community colleges compete with four-year institutions in recruiting new faculty, especially minorities, thereby opening the "window of opportunity" for minority faculty in much the same way it has opened the "door of opportunity" for minority students? The answer is far from clear, but unless major changes take place, success seems highly unlikely.

In the past, community colleges have often been disadvantaged when competing for highly recruited minority faculty. The reasons are obvious: lower faculty salary scales, higher teaching loads, less prestige, fewer opportunities to do research, a more diverse and less academically qualified student body, fewer funds for visiting scholars, and no graduate schools from which to recruit. At Temple University, sixty five African American and Hispanic graduate students who plan to become college professors are provided full financial support. Western Michigan University offers $300,000 worth of assistantships and fellowships to minority graduate students each year.[7] What community college can offer similar incentives to minority students? And how many graduates will settle for teaching at a community college when they will likely have numerous opportunities to teach elsewhere? The community college does indeed face stiff competition in attracting minority faculty members.

A major problem community colleges face in hiring minority faculty members is the dearth of minority role models on community college campuses. Of 619 academic deans responding to a survey sent to the 1,169 chief academic officers of the nation's community colleges, 3.2 percent, or twenty deans were African American; 1.8 percent, or eleven deans, were Hispanic; and 2.0 percent, or twelve deans, were members of other racial or ethnic minority groups.[8] Since the academic deanship is the most common route to becoming a community college president, unless things change it is unlikely that many minorities will assume that important position. In turn, a dearth of minority presidents hinders these colleges in attracting minority faculty members, especially those who aspire to the deanship or presidency.

On the other hand, community colleges offer certain advantages over four-year colleges. First, the community college is a good environment for faculty members who want to concentrate on teaching rather than research and publications. Second, as more and more minorities move through the community college, more and more will feel a need to return "home" to teach. Third, the large percentage of minorities enrolled in community colleges provides an early opportunity to begin recruiting minorities into teaching, especially if minority faculty and administrators are encouraged (and given the time) to serve as mentors. Finally, the over 1,100 community colleges offer fertile fields of opportunity for minorities who want to move through the academic ranks quickly, assume the deanship, and, ultimately, the presidency. This last point, however, is one of the best-kept secrets in all of higher education.

In addition, community colleges can make teaching more attractive for all faculty, thereby enhancing their ability to attract minority faculty. If teaching in the community college is to be accorded the professional status granted to the profession in most four-year institutions, teaching faculty must occupy a more prominent role in providing college-wide leadership. In the past, community colleges have relied almost totally upon administrative leadership in planning the direction of the college; they have not made faculty members full partners in the enterprise. But to rely almost totally on administrators to lead the community college into the next century is to view the issues too narrowly and define leadership too traditionally and exclusively. If teaching in a community college is to be attractive for minorities as well as others, teaching faculty members must not only sit at the table once the meal is ready, they must also be involved in helping to decide what food is to be prepared, when, by whom, and in what form. Teaching faculty can bring experience, knowledge, and compassion to college leadership that will be missing if they are excluded. For example, language and economics teachers can bring their knowledge to the discussion of the community college's role in international education; nursing faculty members could help plan programs dealing with an aging population; counselors could help formulate the college's policy on drugs, and librarians could lead discussions on the utilization and storage of information. The list is endless. The point is, community colleges can make themselves more attractive to faculty and administrators if they utilize their talents to the fullest. If community college leaders, in communicating their mission, can communicate opportunities for teachers and administrators, the chances of recruiting more minority faculty members can be increased.

THE COMMUNITY COLLEGE: SOME ETHICAL CONSIDERATIONS

In chapter 6, the author ventures into the debate on institutional ethics, a debate that has no beginning, no end, and few agreed-upon boundaries. But no matter how complex the issue, the author is correct in discussing ethics, for today no serious discussion of higher education can or should avoid a discussion of ethical issues.

The debate on ethics is hardly new; higher education has traditionally been concerned with values within society and the ethical correctness of its leaders' decisions. Indeed, since the founding of Harvard in 1636, higher education has been a major force in the nation's struggle to establish and maintain high ethical standards. Higher education assumed, or was assigned, the role of interpreting American democracy for a nation that has constantly struggled to practice such (and at times sexually, racially, and culturally biased) concepts as freedom, equality, and justice for all. Much like the established church, higher education has held responsibility for establishing, interpreting, and maintaining ethical standards. The community college, as a part of higher education, must not only enter the debate on ethics, but also define that debate in terms of the community college mission.

Community college leaders, especially presidents, can and should create a campus climate in which decisions are considered from the perspective of what is ethically right. In addition, these decisions should effectively meet societal, institutional, and individual needs while maintaining institutional integrity. This point stems from the belief that rules, regulations, and standards of campus conduct rest on a moral base of commonly accepted concepts of right and wrong, and that all members of the college community are ethically bound by these concepts. By viewing daily decisions from the perspective of what is right and wrong, the campus climate evolves in such a way that ethical considerations become a part of the institution's culture. A culture with roots in the past, extending into the future, is less subject to the daily pressures that often influence the campus climate.

Why should community colleges be concerned with leadership and values more today than in the past? First, society is crying out for some segment of the population to step forward and provide leadership that emphasizes values. Community college leadership is qualified to play this role because of its pragmatic approach to problems, its location within society, and the value it places on education that offers immediate returns for the student and society. Second, community colleges can react to changes and challenges in society more quickly than traditional institutions of higher education. Finally, community colleges, more than any other segment of higher education, occupy that middle ground where higher education and the workplace meet. By reversing the concept of the student as citizen to the concept of citizen as student, community colleges enjoy a unique opportunity to promote ethical values in ways that exert an immediate impact on the daily lives of the citizen-student. By contrast, traditional institutions allow four years (often excusing some rather bizarre violations of ethics along the way) for the student to graduate, enter the workplace, and assume the full rights and responsibilities of citizenship.

By entering the debate on ethics, community colleges have placed themselves squarely in the middle of a larger debate on the role of higher education in a new decade and a new century. As institutions dedicated to serving the local community, community colleges ought to be in the center of this debate. Community college leaders should seize the opportunity to ensure that their colleges build ethical values into their students. Democracy's college can and should do no less.

A CONCLUDING STATEMENT

As the issues facing higher education become more complex and immediate, community college leaders must commit themselves to understanding these issues and working with the rest of higher education to find solutions. Community colleges can be especially helpful in finding ways to educate minorities to fill the many jobs necessary for this nation to compete in the world. One word of caution is in order, however. It should be reemphasized that all minority students must not be channelled into technical fields. The nation must provide opportunities and encouragement for minorities to become doctors, lawyers, professors, or anything else their talents and ambitions will let them become. On the other hand, in communicating the community college mission, community college leaders must illustrate to the individual and society the value of educating a workforce to fill the great void that now exists in technical areas requiring more than a high school diploma and less than a bachelor's degree. Community colleges are uniquely qualified to fill this void. The community college perspective, then, is valuable only when viewed from the perspective of the larger society, the rest of higher education, and the community college mission.

PART TWO

The States and Higher Education

Faced with changing cultural, social, and economic conditions, America's colleges and universities must examine the ways in which they interact with the general public and with elected officials. Institutions of higher education must continually acquire resources from society in order to survive; their very existence and development depend on their stature in the public eye. Consequently, colleges and universities must be concerned with the public trust, i.e, they must maintain positive public opinion by focusing on issues of public and legislative concern.

During the 1980s, attention to educational concerns and financing for educational initiatives shifted from the federal government to the states. In the wake of that transition, college and university administrators have faced new issues, new approaches, and new personalities in governors' offices across the nation. The reason? Governors and state legislators are being held increasingly accountable by a public demanding quality education, while struggling also with significant social issues such as poverty, crime, economic development, health care, and the environment. Convinced that education holds an important key to society's problems, many state leaders are determined to engage a seemingly reluctant academy in the pursuit of solutions.

At the same time, however, colleges and universities are hampered by their nineteenth-century structures and by a thirty-year-old tendency to expect government support on the assumption that everyone considers higher education a worthy cause. Equally troublesome is the trend toward cumbersome bureaucracies at state governance levels, a tendency that denies trust in individual institutions. Without question, institutions will have to work harder to win the trust of the public and their elected leaders in the 1990s. They must communicate better; they must focus on the most important public issues; and, at all costs, they must avoid the business-as-usual syndrome. On the other hand, governors must provide leadership; states must unfetter institutions, allowing them to become entrepreneurial; and multi-campus governing boards must focus on strategic issues rather than attempt to micromanage their institutions.

These challenges are covered in chapters 9–14, collectively titled "The States and Higher Education." Chapter 9 explores tensions between college presidents and proactive governors, offering suggestions for improving these crucial relationships. Chapter 10 further examines the emergence of state governors as educational leaders, profiling four noted governors identified by the 1988–89 CPSE survey and offering hints for other leaders who aspire to improve education in their states. For additional guidance, Chapter 11 analyzes ten leading state university systems, citing characteristics that contribute to excellence. Chapter 12 discusses new approaches to managing postindustrial organizations and recommends colleges and universities as a management model for other societal institutions. Chapter 13 is devoted to two related issues: the calcification of state regulatory boards at a time when change demands flexibility, and the rise of political figures as leaders in American higher education. Chapter 14, the final chapter in this section, offers advice to multicampus governing boards on developing a system-wide strategy building on the strengths of individual institutions, within the context of the multicampus university's overall responsibility to the state and nation.

ILDS

Intersystems Library Delivery Service
Routing Label

Do not remove this label until item reaches destination

Send to: **Lincoln Christian College and Seminary**
The Jessie C. Eury Library
100 Campus View Drive

From: **Lincoln, IL 62656**

Circle destination library's ILDS address:

Alliance LS -4	LCLS -5	SIUE -5
Augustana -4	Loyola U -1B	SIUM -3
BAC - 5	LTLS -3	State Library -3
Bradley U -3	Neastern U -1B	Suburban LS -1A
Chicago LS -1A	NILS -1A	U of Chicago -1B
DePaul U -1B	Northern IL U -1A	UI Peoria -3
DuPage LS -1A	NSLS -1B	UI Rockford -1A
Eastern IL U -3	Nwestern U -1B	UI Urbana -3
Elmhurst Col -1B	Riv Bend LS -4	UIC - LHS -2
Gov State U -2	Rte Cntrl Ofc -2	UIC Main Lib -2
Her Trail LS - 1A	Roosevelt U -1B	UIC RRB -2
IL Inst Tech -1B	Roll Prair LS -3	UIS - 5
IL Wesleyan -3	Shawnee LS -6	Wheaton Col -1B
IL State U -3	SIUC -6	Western IL U -4
Kankakee CC -2		

Notes:

6/95

9

Governors Versus College Presidents: Who Leads?

The 1980s brought fundamental change to America, including a shift of governmental activism from the federal to the state level, i.e., from the president to the governors. Ronald Reagan's ascent to power in 1981, with his determination to trim back the federal government to get it "off the backs of the people," coincided with the emergence of a new breed of governors. Elected in the mid–1970s, the group was epitomized by Robert Graham of Florida, Michael Dukakis of Massachusetts, Lamar Alexander of Tennessee, Thomas Kean of New Jersey, and Bruce Babbitt of Arizona.

This post-Vietnam generation of governors, ambitious and well-educated, leaped at the opportunity to confront social and economic challenges and to establish, in the words of author David Osborne, "laboratories of democracy." Consequently, a time of federal restraint, of shifting and challenging economies, proved to be an era of the "progressive" governor, both Democratic and Republican.

At the same time, American higher education began to confront the effects of the shift from federal to state control. In November 1986, *Washington Post* editorialist Amy Schwartz raised the issue of whether or not universities were acting just like any other insatiable special interest group. She reported growing hostility toward the higher education establishment on the part of Congress, congressional staff, and others in the nation's capital.

Schwartz castigated higher education leaders for their role in the debates surrounding tax reform, mandatory retirement, and government spending. She accused colleges and universities of "not wanting to play by the rules" and "always seeking special treatment," whatever the question.[1]

About the same time, Robert Rosenzweig, president of the prestigious Association of American Universities, commented in an opinion piece for the *Chronicle of Higher Education*:

> Universities are viewed differently from the way they used to be and from the way we view ourselves, and the differences are troublesome. It would be easy to say that we have an "image" problem, but I would prefer to say that we have a reality problem. Much has changed in institutions and the context in which they operate, and those changes are now being felt in the political and policy arenas. It is essential that we understand the fact and govern our individual and collective actions accordingly if we are to retain the confidence on which the future success of universities will depend.[2]

WHO ARE THE GOVERNORS LISTENING TO?

If Rosenzweig was concerned about the serious communications gap between higher education lobbyists (and perhaps universities in general) and the rest of the Washington establishment, including the influential *Post*, he should have attended the Spring 1986 meeting of the state relations committee of the American Association of State Colleges and Universities. After an extensive discussion revealing that few educators were aware of their governors' plans for higher education, one university president blurted out, "Just who are the governors listening to?"

Like their leaders in Washington, these university presidents were confused, even hurt, by their lack of communication with government. The new breed of governors, convinced that higher education, more than ever, would play a crucial role in economic competitiveness in the twenty-first century, were generating their own ideas about the role of colleges and the curricula they should offer. But college presidents felt left out of the decision-making process and the communications loop regarding higher education in their home states.

To explore the question "Who are the governors listening to?" the Center for Policy Study in Education at George Mason University decided to ask the governors. In the summer of 1986, all fifty governors were surveyed; thirty-two provided usable responses. The nine-question survey included such questions as "Where do your best ideas on educational policy come from?" "What educational publications are you most likely to read?" "Which educational meeting are you most likely to attend in a course of a year"? "Which national/regional organizations best serve your needs regarding higher education policy and programs?"

The results of this survey were published by the center in December 1986 in a twelve-page monograph. The following year, over 1000 copies of the document sold. In addition, it was covered in the *Chronicle of Higher Education* and daily newspapers around the country. The findings published in that report are summarized here:

- Governors did not rely on higher education leaders for ideas, programs, and policies for state institutions. In fact, interviews supplemental to the survey revealed governors are generally standoffish toward college and university presidents.
- Governors instead relied on their own people (cabinet officers and special assistants) and organizations (National Governors Association and Education Commission of the States, for example) for issues, ideas, and programs.
- Governors essentially got their ideas from each other, ideas that evolved through a metamorphosis as they were passed around a closed circle of governors and associations.[3]

These "new governors" saw many economic and social problems that could and should be tackled at the state level.* And they were convinced that education holds the key to many doors that must be opened if the United States of America is to enter the twenty-first century as a leading partner in a new world economic order. (In the 1986 survey, twenty-nine of thirty-two governors responding reported education as a top priority of their administrations, and most had been successful in convincing their legislatures to fund educational initiatives.)

Faced with a ticking clock (eight years was the maximum tenure of office for most) the governors of the '80s were action oriented. They wanted to define problems and solutions immediately, during the first year in office, and initiate programs.

Apparently, however, these eager state leaders felt frustrated by a lack of responsiveness on the part of colleges and universities. Not only did they feel their own ideas and initiatives did not move fast enough, they also saw insufficient action on the part of academe in defining and tackling twenty-first century issues and problems. What they did see, however, were requests for more money for generic issues and programs—faculty, salaries, equipment, and de-

*David Osborne notes that national policies of yesteryear, including many of Franklin Roosevelt's initiatives, originated in the states—or "laboratories of democracy" (*Laboratories of Democracy: A New Breed of Governor Creates Models for National Growth*, Boston: Harvard Business School Press, 1988).

ferred maintenance, for example. While governors realize these long-term investments are necessary, they still feel compelled to take immediate action, and do not see much help coming from the academy.

THE PROBLEM GETS WORSE

As a result of this situation, characterized by independent attitudes and actions of governors and puzzlement and irritation by college and university presidents, a serious communications gap between the two camps was identified in 1986. Unfortunately, the 1988–89 CPSE survey of higher education indicated the communications gap had quickly grown into a rift. For example, governors were asked to identify "troubling behavior patterns emerging in the administration of colleges and universities." Their replies highlighted two major topics: (1) incompetency of two-and four-year school administrators, and (2) excessive administrative expenses.

The incompetency response represents a distillation of several statements by governors, including: "lack of concern for quality among college administrators," "lack of clear educational administration," "inability to control costs," "reluctance to be accountable," "mistrust/competition among administrators and institutions," and "competency decline of two- and four-year college administrators." Nineteen of the twenty-six responding governors clearly identified college and university presidents as specific problems contributing to the "incompetency" and "excessive administration expenses."

These responses seem to represent a significant change from the 1986 survey of governors. The discrepancy could be explained, however, by the directness of the 1988–89 question. (The 1986 conclusion was drawn from a series of questions designed to find out where governors were obtaining their ideas on higher education policies and initiatives.)

College and university presidents, on the other hand, responded to this same question very differently. They listed "political interference," "increased regulations," "too much state control," and "not enough attention to the long-term" as "troubling behavior patterns emerging in the administration of colleges and universities." Of sixty-nine college presidents responding to the 1988–89 survey, seven saw no troubling patterns emerging in higher education, but three expressed concern about the quality of two- and four-year college administrators. Twenty-seven presidents saw "externalization" of key administrative decisions as a major problem. And many of those twenty-seven mentioned "political influence" on administrative decisions and "lack of clear direction" from the state as troubling patterns.

The 1988–89 survey did reflect some commonalities in the responses of governors and presidents. Neither, for example, foresaw the growing problem of racial tensions as a difficulty on campuses. And neither mentioned "sharing goals and plans with faculty" as did the other higher education professionals surveyed. But overall survey results clearly indicated that a rift exists between governors and college presidents, a breach that poses a serious problem for colleges and universities in the 1990s.

The responsibility for rectifying this situation must rest on college and university presidents. Granted, college and university presidents, like mayors, corporate officers, union officials, and other leaders in contemporary America, are losing their ability to lead. They are limited by government regulations, by the press, and by organized workers, including faculty, whether unionized or not. And to be sure, college presidents do not elect governors, and governors cannot be ignored or fought. But those in leadership positions must step up to the responsibility to lead.

What can presidents do? An old proverb advises that the way to change other people's behavior is to change your own. This is precisely what college and university presidents must do if they are to be heard as functioning members of their state's leadership team. First, higher education must take seriously the nation's problems: poverty, national competitiveness, environmental questions, national fiscal matters, and minority participation in American life, to list but a few.

Harvard President Derek Bok has long held a leadership role in articulating this view. He insists that colleges and universities can help define and generate ideas for solutions to the nation's problems. He insists also that we not snub applied research, since it is in the application of knowledge that the Japanese and others are outcompeting the United States.

SUGGESTIONS FOR THE HIGHER EDUCATION COMMUNITY

In an era when decisions made at the state capital hold increasing consequences for higher education, the axiom "perception is reality" is an important one for university leaders to remember. If colleges and universities seem detached from state issues and appear preoccupied with their own concerns, if higher education leaders are perceived as approaching the state capital with their hands out, interested only in grabbing the money and running, then why shouldn't governors (and legislators) look to more independent and less self-centered institutions and individuals for ideas, programs, and policies—even in those decisions involving higher education?

If, however, higher education leaders believe it is important to become team members in the global stakes game now underway in the state capitals, new strategies for cooperation must be developed and initiated. However, any such strategies should be built around one overriding principle. The American higher education system is a major national resource, one that must be perceived and used as a primary force for the common good; therefore, college and university leaders must work to include societal needs on the agenda as they go about developing their institutions—and they must be seen to be doing so. To this end, the following recommendations are suggested:

• College and university leaders must pay more attention to broader state issues. Concern with the long-term health of their states—economic, political, social, environmental, as well as educational—should be a constant preoccupation of colleges and their leaders. Without a healthy state, higher education will obviously wither, private institutions hardly less than public ones.

• Colleges and universities possess an enormous capacity for generating new ideas and approaches to state issues and concerns. In many cases, simply alerting faculty that state issues are of concern to their institution's leaders will focus attention on generating relevant ideas. Administrators can stimulate this process by identifying and reinforcing faculty energy devoted to state issues.

In other cases, colleges and universities may want to formally structure such a process through a public policy institute or the like. In addition, in recruiting faculty, institutions can focus preference on individuals with interest and expertise in state issues and policy making.

• An institution's public image can be shaped, in part, by the president's use of the executive office to speak out on public issues. Although they must avoid taking sides on partisan issues, presidents should nevertheless speak out, write newspaper columns, and occasionally communicate privately with state leaders—always seeking to educate and to provide alternatives.

• In their interactions with state governments, colleges and universities should consider a team-oriented approach. Faculty can identify issues, offer ideas, and advise boards, task forces, staffs, and elected officials. Presidents, vice presidents, deans, staff, and board members can all contribute as productive team members by cultivating individual relationships, offering ideas, and gathering information on state issues via contacts with leaders in state government.

• Educators must become involved where education policy changes originate. Consequently, college and university presidents must participate in think tanks studying state issues, and in information exchange forums represented by the Education Commission of the States (ECS), the National Governors' Association, and the Southern Regional Education Board. The dramatic revitalization of ECS during the 1980s emphasized not only the increased importance of the states' role in education matters, but also the intense desire of governors and legislators for information and ideas on higher education.

- More attention must be focused on rapidly developing gubernatorial (and legislative) staffs. Titles may differ—secretary of education, policy analyst, or special assistant—but in almost every state, a new cadre of government professionals is developing. Educators must not underestimate the role and importance of these new technocrats. Not only are these staffers technically competent, they also represent an important link in new information loops developing at the state capitals. Informal loops are equally important to formal ones. Educators must therefore tap into both formal and informal loops.

- College and university leaders should read, discuss and inform those publications read by policy makers instead of those read only by other educators.

- Academic institutions, through various policy centers and departments, can prepare and publish timely articles and books on public issues, including educational issues that state executive and legislative leaders will have to confront. The focus should be on identifying issues, tracing their evolution, and analyzing alternative solutions.

Clearly, basic relationships between public institutions of higher education and their state governments will differ to an important degree in the 1990s. The states have taken on an expanding role in economic development, social programs, and education; a new type of governor—younger, more aggressive, and more determined—is taking charge and making things happen; and, new policy information and decision loops comprising government staff, task forces, and national organizations are taking shape. The combination of these forces means that higher education must create a new leadership role for itself, one that addresses broader social and economic issues at the state level.

Also, in addition to exerting leadership in the pursuit of academic excellence and the control of athletic programs, college and university presidents must stand tall in the state policy arena. If they accept this challenge in a determined and constructive manner, American higher education can take a seat in the new state-level inner circles that are charting America's course for the future. American institutions and society will then reinforce the historic, symbiotic relationship between town and gown, a relationship which mutually benefits and enriches the health and growth of both.

10

Education Governors:
Four Case Studies

In the 1988–89 CPSE study, governors, college and university presidents, and other higher education professionals were asked which governors they would recognize for their efforts to improve the quality of public colleges and universities. Respondents cited former New Jersey Gov. Thomas Kean, Arkansas Gov. Bill Clinton, former Tennessee Gov. Lamar Alexander, and Sen. Robert Graham, former governor of Florida.

A closer look at these four leaders confirms their outstanding contributions to public education, from kindergarten through college, and reveals similarities in their backgrounds and approaches to education. All four men are themselves well educated, holding both bachelor's and advanced degrees from major colleges and universities. Each viewed quality education as a state rather than a federal priority, crucial to economic development. Each acted promptly and aggressively in initiating reform measures, beginning at the elementary and secondary levels. All four men have been active in education reform on a national basis; most have served as leaders of the Education Commission of the States or the National Governors Association. And all four encountered strenuous opposition to their reform proposals, particularly from their state's branch of the National Education Association. Yet in each case, these visionaries persevered in their bold attempts to prepare today's students for life in the twenty-first century.

THOMAS H. KEAN, NEW JERSEY

Few contemporary politicians have championed educational causes with the passion of Thomas H. Kean, former Republican governor of New Jersey and number one on the 1988–89 CPSE survey respondents' list of education governors. "There is no subject more worthy of the attention of political leaders at any level," Kean wrote in 1986, "than the education of our children and the preparation of those who teach them."[1]

In his eight years as governor of New Jersey, Kean proved his commitment to those words. A year after assuming office in 1982, even before the release of "A Nation at Risk," Kean presented to the New Jersey legislature a comprehensive program of educational reform designed to enhance the teaching profession, raise student expectations, and strengthen educational leadership in the state's public schools. Over the next few years, as many of these proposals became law, New Jersey stepped to the forefront of the school reform movement.

At the same time, Kean acted to beef up higher education in New Jersey—raising state funding levels, promoting a $90 million bond issue for new construction and equipment, initiating a competitive grant program to foster innovative institutional projects, and lobbying for more autonomy for colleges and universities in financial matters. Consequently, New Jersey's institutions of higher education—once disdained as second-rate—have gained new nationwide respect. "This is the choice state to be in now for public higher education," commented Harold W. Eickhoff, president of Trenton State College, in 1987.[2]

Kean's devotion to education stems from a profound personal belief in its critical importance. A 1957 graduate of Princeton University, Kean earned a master's degree at Columbia University and taught high-school English and history for three years before his election to the New Jersey legislature, where he served five terms. He later taught political science at Rutgers University and has devoted much of his political career to educational concerns. A former chairman of the Education Commission of the States, Kean also served as cochairman of the National Governors' Association (NGA) committee that published "Time for Results: The Governors' 1991 Report on Education." As a member of the Carnegie Forum on Education and the Economy task force, he contributed to the report "A Nation Prepared: Teachers for the 21st Century." He also served on Princeton University's Board of Trustees and in January 1990 assumed the presidency of Drew University.

Turning visibility into opportunity, Gov. Kean became a frequent author, speaker, and panel member in educational circles, preaching his gospel of reform to all who would listen. Its primary tenets included: a national board of professional standards for teachers; an overhaul of teacher education; constructive collaboration among teachers, school boards and administrators; district-based regulatory systems; and more thoughtful teacher recruitment and retention programs.

Kean also promoted the "Governors' Action Agenda" developed by the NGA Task Force on Teaching, maintaining that gubernatorial support is essential to progress in education reform. To create a "new compact between the public and teachers," Kean recommended that governors:

1. Convene a statewide panel to review the national teacher policy reports
2. Support the creation of a national board of professional teacher standards
3. Develop state initiatives to encourage professional school environments
4. Challenge the higher education community on teacher education
5. Build the case for sustained increases in real dollars spent on education
6. Define and establish a comprehensive teacher recruitment strategy
7. Announce the end of emergency teaching licenses, which allow unqualified people to teach
8. Listen to teachers, principals, board members, and others, for new ideas and to focus energy and commitment
9. Recognize outstanding teaching
10. Establish a state intervention procedure as a last resort in cases of intractable school failure

Many of these recommendations are now in force in New Jersey as a result of legislative reforms first proposed by Kean in 1983. To ensure a statewide pool of qualified and committed faculty, the state developed new programs to recruit, develop, and reward outstanding teachers. A 1985 minimum salary law brought starting pay for New Jersey teachers from less than $15,000 to $18,500. And, in 1986, the Governor's Teaching Scholars program began offering top high school graduates college scholarship loans, forgivable in exchange for service in New Jersey public schools.

At the same time, the state eliminated emergency teaching credentials, upped academic standards, and lowered the proportion of education courses required during teacher training in New Jersey colleges. New teachers must now hold bachelor's degrees and pass competency tests. In addition, New Jersey pioneered an alternate route to teacher certification for professionals who meet these criteria and complete a one-year teaching internship. And, to keep its existing public faculty and administrators, the state now offers professional development programs, grants to implement innovative classroom strategies, and cash awards for teaching excellence.

Other New Jersey reforms focused on raising academic standards for students by adopting new course requirements and proficiency tests necessary for high school graduation. In addition, stringent codes of conduct and alternative school programs for chronically disruptive and emotionally handicapped students have aimed at improving student behavior. To provide an incentive for more students to graduate, the state joined with New Jersey businesses to initiate a job placement program for urban high school graduates. And to combat illiteracy, the state developed a volunteer network of literacy tutors. Other new laws provided for school monitoring and state intervention in chronically deficient school districts.

Additional school innovations either adopted or under consideration in New Jersey include a parent involvement program, prekindergarten classes, improved vocational education and special education curricula, and funding incentives for particularly effective schools.

To strengthen educational leadership, New Jersey reorganized its Department of Education in 1983 and has since reexamined certification requirements for principals, school business officials and district superintendents. The state has also provided special assistance to urban schools and devised a plan for instructional supervision.

Though concentrating on reforms for New Jersey's public school system, Kean never lost sight of the needs of higher education, for reasons he outlined in a 1985 essay for the *Chronicle of Higher Education*:

> This nation should be as deeply concerned about the quality of undergraduate education as it has been, over the last few years, about the quality of public-school education. The often-stated view that we have the best higher-education system in the world is beside the point. The system is no longer sufficient, not because its quality has declined, but because our need for it has expanded so dramatically... What is at stake is not only economic renewal but also the capacity for true resurgence in all dimensions of our personal, civic, and cultural life.[3]

Kean emphasized the state's role in higher education in a 1985 interview with *Change* magazine, noting that its many problems "aren't going to get solved at any other level of government except the state level."[4]

"Governors and legislators are recognizing the fact that a strong educational presence is of tremendous benefit to a state's prestige, economy, and quality of life," Kean explained. "Then there's the simple fact that states pay for most of higher education."[5]

Kean's prescription for colleges and universities rests on his assumption that "excellence in higher education requires excellent institutional leadership"[6] and that states must contribute to a climate that encourages faculty and administrators to implement their own ideas to improve their individual institutions. "The key . . . is to find an appropriate balance between state leadership and support on one hand and institutional autonomy on the other," Kean said.[7] To meet this goal, Kean suggested that state leaders support the initiatives of higher education leaders, focus public attention on the importance of improving higher education, move the state's relationship with colleges from one of control to empowerment, and push institutional leaders to devise methods of assessing their progress.

In New Jersey, Kean has pushed for implementation of these objectives. The state's competitive grant programs, designed to finance innovative programs at both private and public universities and to assist institutions in developing an academic expertise, are regarded by some as models for the nation.[8] Under new state laws, New Jersey's public institutions now conduct their own purchasing and set their own tuition rates. Additional programs have focused on increasing minority enrollments and encouraging a comprehensive plan for assessment of institutional performance. Meanwhile, the New Jersey Commission on Science and Technology, a blend of public sector and private industry representatives, assigned five state universities to conduct research in specified growth industries for the state. All these initiatives fit into Kean's overall plan to weave higher education into New Jersey's economic and social fabric.

Though not without his detractors, Kean has met with resounding approval as New Jersey's "education governor." It's a role he justifies easily. "Any state that aspires to leadership," Kean says, "has to have strong education."[9]

BILL CLINTON, ARKANSAS

In 1978, a study commissioned by the Arkansas General Assembly declared that state's public schools the worst in the nation. "From an educational standpoint," the report said, *the average child in Arkansas would be much better off attending the public schools of almost any other state in the country.*"[10] But within a decade, Arkansas emerged as a premiere example of the school reform movement that swept the nation in the wake of "A Nation at Risk." In large measure, the driving force behind this transformation was Arkansas Governor and Democratic presidential contender Bill Clinton.

In 1983, within a year of beginning his second term as governor (he sat out a two-year term due to a 1980 election defeat), Clinton championed a package of controversial and far-reaching education reform legislation. In 1989, following tough skirmishing with Arkansas legislators, he won partial approval of a second wave of reform proposals designed to further the state's educational ascent.

Clinton's resume reflects both personal and public commitment to education. An Arkansas native, he is a 1968 graduate of Georgetown University and a 1973 graduate of Yale University Law School; he also studied at England's Oxford University as a Rhodes scholar. In 1986, he became the first individual to simultaneously chair both the Education Commission of the States and the National Governors' Association. A frequent speaker and author on education, he presented "Speaking of Leadership," a report on the importance of leadership in education reform, to the Education Commission in July 1987.

Clinton's Arkansas reform engine started even before the release of "A Nation at Risk" and gained speed despite looming revenue shortfalls and a state supreme court ruling dubbing the state's distribution of education funds "inequitable." Further threatening the governor's plans, the Arkansas Education Association, the state's biggest union, reacted strongly to Clinton's proposal for teacher competency testing. Convinced the governor was focusing blame on teachers for political purposes, the group marshalled formidable opposition to the measure and managed to win its repeal in the House, but not the Senate.

The 1983 reform package grew from recommendations of the newly created Education Standards Committee, chaired by Yale University law graduate and Arkansas First Lady Hillary Clinton. The new laws mandated pay hikes and competency tests for teachers; a longer school day and year; smaller classes; high school admissions tests for eighth graders; raising the dropout age from fifteen to sixteen; stricter requirements for high school graduation; expanded course offerings in science, math, computers, arts, music, foreign languages, and gifted education—and a one-cent hike in the state sales tax to fund it all.

But lawmakers refused Clinton's proposed hike in corporate and severance tax rates, designed to raise funds for higher education. In a compromise agreement, three-fourths of the increased sales tax revenues were set aside for public schools and the remaining one-fourth was earmarked for post-secondary education, including higher education, adult education and vocational-technical training. Improvements included new college and university science and engineering facilities, scholarships, and student loans. By 1987, the $168 million annual hike in funding effected an 88 percent increase in state aid to public schools and raised the state's investment in all levels of education to seventy cents per tax dollar.[11]

In the first six years after the initial reforms were enacted, Arkansas' high school graduation rate rose from 73.4 percent to 77.5 percent,[12] the South's highest.[13] And the proportion of Arkansas students entering college increased from 38.7 percent in 1982, to 44.5 percent in 1989.[14] In addition, enrollment in advanced math and computer science courses tripled, partly because of the first-time availability of advanced courses in all Arkansas schools. Annual basic skills testing charted a steady rise in reading and math scores.

A key result of Clinton's reforms came in the area of college preparation. Before 1983, many of the state's small and impoverished rural school districts did not even offer the necessary courses for college admission, leaving about a third of the state's high school valedictorians ineligible for admission to certain Arkansas colleges except on probationary status. By 1987, following mergers and consolidations that eliminated forty school districts, every district in the state offered the full complement of college preparation courses, as well as additional classes in computer science and the arts.

After the initial surge of education reform, Clinton continued to push for ongoing improvements, particularly in the area of leadership. "Strong leaders create strong schools," he wrote in a 1986 *Phi Delta Kappan* article. "Our challenge now is to develop state policies that strengthen school leadership and encourage school renewal."[15]

Clinton's suggestions for tackling this challenge at the state level included matching state-sponsored educational training and certification requirements to the skills required by effective principals, providing incentives and technical assistance to foster school-site management and renewal, and developing a system of evaluation and rewards for principals.

Following high-level critiques of Arkansas' system of public institutions in the late 1980s, Clinton also proposed further changes for colleges and universities. They included: eliminating duplicate academic programs, capping college athletic department deficits, promoting increased attendance at two-year community colleges, seeking performance reviews of all college faculty, doubling state funding for scholarships, raising faculty salaries to regional parity, and providing grants for minority teacher trainees.

Clinton's reform philosophy hinges on the link between education and economic development. "This country is in a period of profound economic change," he said in a September 1986 interview with the *Chronicle of Higher Education.* "With the growth in the international economy, people are taking a beating in the trade market. To have real economic growth, we're going to have to produce more better-educated people."[16]

Clinton's repeated mention of the education/economy link proved persuasive in winning the 1983 sales tax hike, and he continued to press for a second one-cent sales tax hike in 1989. But stiff opposition in the legislature prevented introduction of the new tax proposal and limited further reforms to those not requiring additional funding. They included: statewide school choice; rural magnet schools; mandatory kindergarten; forced mergers of consistently substandard schools; revocation of driving licenses for school dropouts aged seventeen and under; funding to aid disadvantaged students; fines for parents who fail to attend parent-teacher conferences or allow their children to skip school; a minimum teacher salary of $16,000; college tuition savings bonds and annual performance reviews for all college professors; and new laws to strengthen the fight against drugs and violence in schools. In addition, legislators created, but did not fund, a state office to issue annual school report cards.

Clinton also favored faculty salary raises; more college scholarships and work-study programs; a statewide preschool program; expanded children's health services; expanded adult education programs; and college-level research and economic development programs. These measures, however, were not adopted.

Intent on completing his proposed reforms, in September 1989 Clinton began a statewide series of "Education Summits," call-in broadcasts, and newspaper questionnaires to solicit citizen opinion and raise support for continuing education gains.

"I want to determine what still needs to be done," Clinton said, "what can be done with existing revenues and whether the public and the Legislature will support a modified proposal to raise more money for schools."[17]

LAMAR ALEXANDER

During Tennessee's 1978 gubernatorial campaign, Republican candidate Lamar Alexander walked the state in a 1,022-mile, four-month bid for votes that took him into the homes and schools of hundreds of Tennesseeans. Alexander's long journey paid off, bringing him an election victory, plus the conviction that something had to be done to improve the sorry state of public education in Tennessee.

During his first term as governor, Alexander introduced a "Basic Skills First" program in more than 600 elementary schools state-wide. In 1983, after becoming the first Tennessee governor to win election to successive four-year terms, Alexander recommended a sweeping "Better Schools" agenda. The ten-point proposal hinged on the revolutionary concept of a "career ladder" offering recognition and merit pay to outstanding public school teachers. Lamar Alexander's campaign to improve Tennessee's schools proved a tougher political battle than winning the governorship. After more than a year of opposition, delays and compromises, Alexander won only a watered-down version of his career ladder. But the changes were enough to catapult the Tennessee governor to the ranks of state school reformers.

Alexander's interest in education dates back to his earliest years—both his parents were teachers. An eighth-generation Tennessean, Alexander grew up in Marysville, graduated Phi Beta Kappa from Vanderbilt University, and earned a law degree from New York University. Alexander returned to Tennessee in 1970 and ran unsuccessfully for governor in 1974 before his election four years later at the age of thirty-eight. In 1988, he was named president of the University of Tennessee system. Also in that year, he was recognized by the Education Commission of the States for "distinguished national leadership in education." In addition, Alexander serves as a member of President Bush's Education Policy Advisory Committee.

Alexander launched his $1 billion "Better Schools" reform package in the face of rampant poverty and unemployment. (In 1983 Tennessee ranked among the bottom ten states in the nation in per capita income and among the top ten in unemployment rates.)[18] His simple rationale: better schools mean better jobs. Alexander's overall plan for school reform in Tennessee called for "basic skills first, computer skills next, then new job skills for all Tennesseans of all ages."[19] Proposals included mandatory kindergarten, gifted education, more math and science, alternative schools for disruptive students, centers of excellence at universities, more money for books and supplies, plus a new library for the University of Tennessee at Knoxville. But central to all was the Master Teacher Program, the career ladder with merit pay for successful teachers. "Unless we find a way to attract and keep the best teachers," Alexander said, "the rest won't amount to anything. Teachers are the heart of the matter."[20]

The original career ladder concept, presented to the Tennessee legislature in January 1983, called for annual salary increases ranging from $1,000 to $7,000, depending on career level and peer evaluations. Derived from recommendations by the legislature's Comprehensive Education Study, the proposal outlined four career steps for teachers—apprentice, professional, senior, and master teacher—with accompanying three- or five-year certificates at each level. Similar incentives were proposed for principals, supervisors, and other administrators. The bill established a state-run teacher evaluation system to avoid local bias, and limited the number of top level teachers (both statewide and by districts) to keep costs down and ensure even distribution of talented teachers.

Some lawmakers protested the cost of the program and the one-cent sales tax hike Alexander proposed to cover it. Still, the governor was able to muster bipartisan support for his program, despite a two-to-one Democrat to Republican disadvantage in the legislature. But he encountered daunting resistance from the powerful Tennessee Education Association (TEA). TEA members objected strenuously to the career ladder, which they saw as a threat to tenure, due process, and collective bargaining. They complained about the lack of a significant pay raise for all teachers and objected to an untried, but mandatory evaluation process. With the TEA fuming and no grassroots support forthcoming from parents and other citizens, legislators tabled the "Better Schools" program in April 1983.

The package might easily have died at that point, except for the timely release of "A Nation at Risk." In the ensuing concern over school quality, Alexander emerged as a visionary and national spokesman for school reform. The next March, the Tennessee legislature narrowly passed the sales tax hike to finance Alexander's merit pay career ladder. But continued opposition from the TEA resulted in last minute compromises that substantially weakened the original proposals. Hefty pay raises were approved for all teachers, regardless of performance; no caps were placed on the number of top level teachers; and the evaluation system was split between local and state control. Teacher titles were eliminated, but tenure was not, making it difficult to fire incompetent teachers.

"I've run for office three times," commented a shell-shocked Alexander, "but nothing compares to this. It's by far the most difficult thing I've ever been through in my life."[21]

Alexander battled also to improve Tennessee's colleges and universities, which until the mid-1980s ranked at or near the bottom of all fifty states by nearly every criterion.[22] The Alexander administration's proposals to benefit higher education included several successful initiatives. Through its innovative performance funding program, begun in 1979, Tennessee now compensates its colleges and universities for improvements in programs and student achievement with monetary incentives. In addition, the state has invested

$43 million to help endow more than seventy-five professorships or chairs of excellence.[23] Combined with private contributions, these funds work to attract eminent scholars to state institutions. With the goal of elevating chosen programs at each campus to national prominence, Tennessee has also devoted $100 million since 1984 to establish thirty Centers of Excellence designed to promote advanced scholarship in basic and applied research or creative endeavors in the arts.[24] These centers rely on government and private grants and contracts, in addition to state funds. Overall, state funding for higher education increased 50 percent during 1984–1987, the last three years of Alexander's tenure as governor.[25]

Other advancements in higher education during the Alexander administration involved changes at the high school level. Both state university system boards, the University of Tennessee Board and the Board of Regents, enacted tougher admission standards for state colleges and universities. State-funded scholarships were established to encourage promising Tennessee high school graduates to choose Tennessee state colleges. And each summer, Tennessee campuses now offer special instruction to teachers and outstanding high school students at a number of Governor's Schools.

Largely as a result of these reforms, Tennessee's state institutions of higher education have risen to average national ranking. "In the 80s, we experienced the most significant turnaround in higher education in the history of the state," said Arliss Roaden, executive director of the Tennessee Higher Education Commission, in a December 1989 interview with the *Nashville Tenneseean*. "What we have done is move from the cellar up to be competitive at the average. Now it is our challenge to move from being average up to being among the leaders."[26] In addition to his statehouse efforts toward educational reform, Alexander served as chairman of the National Governors' Association. In that capacity, he initiated the NGA study "Time for Results: The Governors' 1991 Report on Education." The report recommended career-ladder salary systems; state-run leadership programs for school leaders; school choice; school report cards; state takeovers of chronically deficient schools; year-round use of school facilities; state-sponsored preschool programs; better use of technology in teaching; and student assessment at the college level.

"Governors are ready for some old-fashioned horse trading," Alexander declared in April 1987. "We'll regulate less, if schools and school districts will produce better results." The remarks reflect Alexander's belief that state support is necessary to ensure school reform, but changes must ultimately come from within each institution.[27]

Alexander has also gone on record suggesting that each community set goals for its schools; university faculty become involved in local school curricula; high school and college entrance requirements be stricter; management techniques be applied to teaching to maximize teaching time; and proven leaders—even from fields outside education—be considered as school administrators. A champion of teacher recognition, Alexander advocates titles, honorary degrees, community prestige, and secretaries for teachers, as well as meaningful summer employment and career mobility, both in and out of the teaching profession.

In his new role as president of the University of Tennessee system, Alexander has continued to persevere despite criticism. Though many complained that, without a Ph.D., he lacked the proper academic credentials for the job, Alexander has taken his "better schools mean better jobs" gospel to the university campuses and to the White House as an adviser to President Bush.

"I think 'better schools' is central to any sensible Republican message because Republicans profess to believe that this is a country of opportunity rather than government help," Alexander explained in a June 1988 interview. "And that what we want to do is give people a chance to move from the back of the line to front of the line by their own efforts. The way you do that in America is through education."[28]

ROBERT GRAHAM

In 1982, a year before the official start of the school reform era, United States Senator Robert Graham, then the Democratic governor of Florida and one of the earliest proponents of education reform, sounded the dual alarm of shrinking economic and educational strength.

"We are slowly beginning to realize that in the long run, without a healthy educational system, fundamental economic recovery and industrial revitalization will not take place," Graham said.[29]

Graham stressed that the internationalization of our economy, its shift from an industrial to an information base, and the rapidity of change constituted crucial forces threatening the nation's supremacy as an industrial nation.

"These problems can only be solved by a concerted and sustained effort of government, education, and business and industry," Graham said. "The states, in particular, must take an active role in fostering change if America is to survive in the twenty-first century."[30]

Graham's words followed action. Convinced of education's crucial role in society, Graham and his Cabinet, acting as Florida's State Board of Education, had in 1981 set a goal for the state: "On a statewide average, educational achievement in the State of Florida will equal that of the upper quartile of states within five years, as indicated by commonly accepted criteria of attainment."[31]

By 1984, the United States Department of Education recognized Florida as first in the nation in its progress toward school reform goals set by the National Commission on Excellence in Education in its startling report "A Nation At Risk." Florida had enacted sixteen of the commission's twenty recommendations, including stricter high school graduation requirements, a longer school day, teacher pay raises, and more stringent teacher certification standards.[32]

Graham's push for educational reform continued a long-term personal commitment to educational excellence. Born in Coral Gables in 1936, the son of Florida pioneers—cattleman, developer, and state senator Ernest Graham and schoolteacher Hilda Simmons Graham—Robert Graham graduated Phi Beta Kappa from the University of Florida in 1959. Three years later he received a law degree from Harvard. Graham and his wife Adele Khoury Graham are the parents of four daughters.

In addition to working as a builder and cattleman, Graham served in the Florida House of Representatives and later the Florida Senate, where he became known as a champion for education and the environment. Author of a successful bill requiring competency testing in public schools, Graham also sponsored numerous educational improvement bills as well as a constitutional amendment to expand construction of higher education facilities.

Following his election as governor of Florida in 1979, Graham continued to push for educational reform, both on the state and national levels. He served as chairman of the Education Commission of the States, the Southern Regional Educational Board, the National Advisory Commission on School Finance, and the United States Intergovernmental Advisory Council on Education. In 1986, Graham was elected to represent Florida in the United States Senate.

During Graham's tenure as governor of Florida, the state increased its share of funding for public schools and student performance—from elementary grades to college level—began to register a steady improvement. A case in point: The percentage of community college and lower division university students passing the College Level Academic Skills test required before beginning upper division studies rose from 64 percent in 1982 to more than 89 percent in 1985. In addition, average SAT scores and the number of National Merit Scholars attending Florida's state universities increased steadily during the Graham administration.[33]

Instrumental to Florida's sweeping educational reforms was a united coalition of state legislators who, in 1983, declared the quality of public education Agenda Item Number One. Coalition members helped to obtain funding for key reforms, including longer school days, reduced class sizes, and emphasis on kindergarten through third grade as a critical learning period. Community support for legislative reform efforts was spearheaded by Education Means Business, a coalition of business people who orchestrated and funded an advertising campaign designed to inform Florida citizens of the need for school reform. In addition, corporate sponsors and chambers of commerce have donated equipment, financial resources, and personnel time to help initiate and strengthen local school programs designed to introduce students to economics and career options.

As in Tennessee, a crucial component of Florida's 1983 reform package was a merit pay plan for teachers. As in Tennessee also, the state's "Master Teacher Program" triggered vigorous protest from opponents critical of untested evaluation procedures. But many of these detractors responded positively to Graham's 1986 modifications that replaced merit pay with minimum teacher salaries and expanded the concept to a three-rung career ladder, enabling more teachers to participate.

To pay for its education reforms, Florida increased the corporate income tax. In 1985, the state spent approximately $3 billion on public education, putting Florida thirteenth in the nation (adjusting for cost-of-living) in per-pupil spending for that year. Average Florida teacher salaries (adjusted for cost-of-living) ranked twenty-second nationally at $22,475.[34]

Graham's mandates for educational reform included a special concern for higher education. "This is not the time to move at a snail's pace," he declared in 1981 to a group of influential leaders meeting to discuss future directions for Florida's state university system. "We must unleash the university system from those time-bound constraints which would allow only gradual change."[35]

The accelerated rate of social change demands innovative response, Graham argued, pointing out that Florida's recent rapid growth had provided a window of opportunity for the state's university system to match the pace of the nation's finest public universities.[36]

Graham's counsel found an eager audience. As a result of legislation enacted during his administration, Florida's high school graduation requirements are now among the strictest in the nation. Admission into Florida's state university system requires four foreign language credits, six hours of college-level mathematics and at least twelve hours of courses emphasizing writing skills. Further, students must write at least twenty-four thousand words during these twelve hours of study.[37]

To bolster university faculty ranks, the Florida Legislature established Florida's Eminent Scholars program, including more than eighty chairs, each backed by a $1 million endowment. Among the top experts recruited to fill these positions were Joseph Papp of the New York Shakespeare Festival and renowned economist Henri Theil.

Throughout his tenure as governor, Graham continued to call for more improvements, including more pay, recognition, and career variety for teachers; scholarship incentives to attract top students to teaching; alternate certification procedures to allow for second-career teachers; innovation and excellence in the classroom; reinforced standards and accountability for teacher and administrator performance; and state funding support for educational advancement.

By 1986, when Robert Graham announced his plans to run for the United States Senate against Republican incumbent Paula Hawkins, he had earned the support of the Florida Education Association-United. FEAU president Pat Tornillo explained: "No other governor in the history of the state of Florida has ever placed education as a No. 1 priority and raised the consciousness of the citizenry of Florida as Bob Graham has done."[38]

11

Secrets of the Best State University Systems

States with the best public universities share significant characteristics, according to the 1988–89 CPSE survey of American higher education. Survey results indicate that the ten top-ranked states exhibit a number of similarities involving the efficacy of governance structures, faculty salaries, research expenditures, the number of doctorates awarded, minority and out-of-state enrollments, and state and local funding levels. Taken as a whole, these factors paint a portrait of achievement illustrating the nation's finest public systems of higher education.

PUBLIC UNIVERSITY SYSTEMS RANKED BY STATE

Respondents to the 1988–89 CPSE survey indicated that California, North Carolina, and Michigan operate the nation's top public institutions. Also ranked among the top ten (listed in alphabetical order) were Florida, Illinois, Minnesota, New York, Texas, Virginia, and Wisconsin. Other states with significant survey support included Arizona, Iowa, Massachusetts, New Jersey, Ohio, and Washington. (These rankings are important only as indicators of significant public policy implications.)

The 1988–1989 results were consistent with previous CPSE survey findings, which ranked California, North Carolina, and Michigan among the top four states leading the way in public education in 1987–88. The major difference between the two surveys was that

New York, ranked second in 1987–1988, dropped significantly in 1988–1989. This discrepancy is probably a function of changes within the respondent pool. In 1987–1988, only university presidents were polled, while in 1988–1989, governors and other higher education professionals were added to the list. In the most recent survey, as in the previous poll, college presidents tended to give New York high marks, even though the 1988–1989 respondent pool differed from the 1987–1988 pool in at least three respects: (1) both community college and private college presidents were included among 1988–1989 respondents; (2) significant turnover had occurred among public university presidents; and (3) even among the continuing presidents, some who responded in 1987–1988 failed to do so in 1988–1989, while others who did not reply previously did respond to the later survey.

QUESTIONING A TRADITIONAL INDICATOR OF QUALITY

Contrary to conventional wisdom, one characteristic not shared by the top ten states is governance structure. Among the top three state higher education systems identified in the 1988–1989 CPSE survey, Michigan is highly decentralized, North Carolina is highly centralized, and California falls somewhere between the two. In fact, as the following list indicates, the survey reflected little direct correlation between any state's governance structure and respondents' perceptions of system quality in that state.

States with significant central control
New York
North Carolina
Wisconsin
Florida

States with moderate statewide control
California
Minnesota
Texas
Illinois

States with limited control at the state level
Michigan
Virginia

Significant differences among respondents' preferences existed even within these general categories of state control. For example, North Carolina, ranked number two in the nation, and New York, which placed in the top ten, share similar high levels of central governance, with New York exerting even more state control than North Carolina. Yet, despite the disadvantages of heavy state control, college and university presidents seemed to favor the New York system, while governors and others preferred the less rigid environment of North Carolina.

On the other hand, North Carolina and Virginia operate under very different governance structures, but conform in terms of the character of their individual institutions. Only one board of governors manages North Carolina's thirteen four-year universities, while fourteen boards, plus a weak state coordinating board, operate Virginia's fifteen four-year institutions. Yet, the University of North Carolina at Chapel Hill and the University of Virginia at Charlottesville share many common characteristics, as do North Carolina State and Virginia Tech, and Appalachian State and James Madison. (One major difference between higher education institutions in the two states is that Virginia does not have a large nationally ranked private research university such as Duke or Wake Forest.)

Thus, it is difficult to identify type of governance or level of state control as a significant factor in the perceived quality of a state's higher education system. Clearly, governance structure is not by itself the key to developing a respected system of public education.

EFFECTIVE CONTROL AT THE TOP

A growing consensus, however, indicates that *better* control of a state's university system opens the way to higher quality. Maryland and Oregon present two outstanding examples that support this claim. Each state effected significant and promising changes in the management of its university system—Maryland through centralization and Oregon through limited access.

In 1988, to create a higher education system that would effect greater impact on his state's cultural and economic growth, Maryland Gov. William Donald Schaefer proposed a reorganization designed to bring all state-supported, four-year colleges and universities under the control of the University of Maryland Board of Regents. Schaefer asked the General Assembly for a state commission to coordinate Maryland's university system, community colleges, and private institutions. In addition, he requested a governor-appointed, cabinet-level executive officer for higher education. To expedite his proposal, Schaefer promised a special $50 million higher education appropriation as incentive.

Ultimately, the governor got what he wanted, though with two exceptions. Two schools—historically black Morgan State University and small, specialized St. Mary's College—flexed political muscles strong enough to protect their independence, including individual boards of trustees. In addition, within the expanded system, campus presidents received a new degree of freedom that exceeded Schaefer's original plan.

Though still in its shakedown period, Maryland's newly organized system of higher education appears headed toward a promising future. The change resulted in a fresh infusion of money and a proactive new Board of Regents. In addition, individual campuses now enjoy greater autonomy than in either of two previous systems. The major transition problems at this writing are merging staff members between the old and new systems, defining the goals of the new Board of Regents, and the selection of a new system chancellor.

Unlike in Maryland, Oregon's higher education system had long been governed by a single board. However, on taking office in 1987, Gov. Neil Goldschmidt voiced his frustration that Oregon's colleges and universities did not command the prominence of universities in neighboring California or Washington. After only a short period in office, the new governor moved to change the system. Despite widespread criticism, he secured the resignation of the system chancellor, and by 1988, with four new appointments, took control of the Board of Higher Education. The board then quickly selected a new chancellor, a man with connections to Goldschmidt who won the governor's praise by cutting enrollments—and costs—throughout the university system in order to fund educational improvements.

If new money can build quality—and many believe money is a key factor—both Maryland and Oregon should be successful in their efforts to improve their university systems. Most observers agree that both these states will soon realize progress in terms of conventional measures of quality. In each case, however, progress carried a price tag: the character and mission of higher education in both Maryland and Oregon has been fundamentally changed.

THE BENEFITS OF A STRONG LEAD UNIVERSITY

In Virginia, the perceived quality of the university system remains high despite a governance structure that fosters tensions between state administrators and university faculty. Virginia institutions are constantly battling takeover attempts by the State Council of Higher Education (the state coordinating board). Though prohibited by law from interfering in admissions and faculty decisions, and restricted to minimum involvement in curriculum decisions, state staff intermittently attempt an incursion into these areas, only to be beaten back by University of Virginia faculty.

Virginia's success in achieving high standards of educational quality despite tensions between institutions and the state governance system suggests that the strength of a nationally ranked lead university, such as the University of Virginia, may be an important factor in overall system development. In fact, nine of the top ten states in this ranking can boast of an exceptionally strong lead university. These institutions include the University of California at Berkeley and Los Angeles, the University of North Carolina at Chapel Hill, the University of Texas at Austin, the University of Illinois, the University of Wisconsin at Madison, the University of Florida, the University of Michigan, the University of Minnesota, and the University of Virginia. New York is an exception; it lacks a single lead university, but relies on major research institutions at Albany, Buffalo, Binghamton, and Stoneybrook.

OTHER POSSIBLE FACTORS CONTRIBUTING TO SYSTEM QUALITY

Beyond governance issues, the 1988–89 CPSE study revealed several indicators that relate to system quality, including minority enrollments; out-of-state enrollments and migration; average faculty salaries in public four-year institutions; research expenditures per faculty member; the status of graduate education, in terms of the number of doctorates awarded per year; and revenues per full-time equivalent student from state and local appropriations. Tables 11.1–11.8, taken from the *1986–1987 Fact Book on Higher Education*,[1] explore each of these factors more closely:

T A B L E 11.1. *Minority Enrollments*

20 percent or more:	North Carolina
5–19 percent:	California
	Texas
	Michigan
	Illinois
	New York
	Virginia
	Florida
Less than 5 percent:	Minnesota
	Wisconsin

T A B L E 11.2.   *Enrollment of Out-Of-State Undergraduates*

Less than 15 percent:	California
	Illinois
	Michigan
	North Carolina
	Wisconsin
	Texas
More than 15 percent:	Florida
	Minnesota
	Virginia

T A B L E 11.3.   *Migrations of Undergraduates Out-Of-State*

Less than 15 percent:	California
	Florida
	Illinois
	Michigan
	North Carolina
	New York
	Texas
More than 15 percent:	Minnesota
	Wisconsin
	Virginia

T A B L E 11.4.   *Average Faculty Salaries at Public Four-Year Universities*

California	$39,636
New York	36,879
Minnesota	34,404
Michigan	34,268
Illinois	32,488
Wisconsin	31,736
Virginia	31,638
North Carolina	31,444
Texas	31,311
Florida	29,526

T A B L E 11.5. *Research Expenditures Per Full-Time Faculty Member*

STATE	AMOUNT	RANK IN NATION
California	$24,894	10
Wisconsin	23,743	14
Minnesota	22,261	16
Florida	19,883	18
Michigan	19,743	20
New York	17,729	27
Illinois	17,334	28
Texas	16,666	31
Virginia	14,661	40
North Carolina	14,292	41

T A B L E 11.6. *Doctoral Degrees Awarded by State*

700 OR MORE DOCTORATES	LESS THAN 700
California	Minnesota
Florida	Virginia
Illinois	Wisconsin
Michigan	
North Carolina	
New York	
Texas	

T A B L E 11.7. *Institutions Offering the Doctoral Degree*

TEN OR MORE	FIVE TO NINE
California	Minnesota
Florida	North Carolina
Illinois	Virginia
Michigan	Wisconsin
New York	
Texas	

TABLE 11.8.   *State and Local Appropriations Per Full-Time-Equivalent Student*

California	$4,411
Texas	4,325
North Carolina	4,165
Wisconsin	3,886
Virginia	3,646
Florida	3,601
New York	3,286
Michigan	3,276
Minnesota	3,037
Illinois	2,882

SURVEY CONCLUSIONS

As outlined above, the 1988–1989 survey results do not indicate that unusual minority enrollment patterns help determine the relative respect a state system of higher education enjoys. Most university systems in the top ten report moderate (5 to 19 percent) enrollment of minority students.

On the other hand, the above data clearly dispel a common belief that large out-of-state undergraduate enrollments signal educational quality. Seven of the ten top-ranked states, including the top three—California, North Carolina, and Michigan, register less than 15 percent out-of-state undergraduates in their institutions. Perhaps more significant is the finding that only three of the ten top states—Minnesota, Virginia, and Wisconsin—see more than 15 percent out-of-state migration.

In addition, this study identifies only six states that rank among the nation's top twenty-five institutions in terms of research dollars per student, suggesting the quality of a state's research institutions does not significantly affect its overall reputation. The production of doctorates, however, definitely registers as a dominant factor in the perception of educational quality. Seven of the ten top-ranked states award 700 or more doctorates per year, while only three award less than 700.

In terms of dollars per student gleaned from state and local appropriations, seven of the ten leading states identified in this study rank among the top twenty nationwide. At the same time, seven of the ten register among the top twenty states in terms of average faculty salary in four-year public institutions, indicating salary levels are another important factor when assessing the quality of a state system.

A PROFILE OF ACHIEVEMENT

The above data suggest a composite profile of achievement for state systems held in high esteem by the respondents of the 1988–1989 CPSE survey. Notable characteristics shared by a majority of the leading state systems include:

significant minority enrollments
low in-state and out-of-state migration
high priority set on faculty salaries
support for faculty research
strong doctoral institutions and enrollments
good state and local financial support

Though these attributes can be established as institutional goals, progress toward meeting these objectives is no guarantee of success. Further, tactics such as changing governance structure are not a panacea for improving a state's higher education system.

The success of these outstanding systems is to a large degree a function of perspective or mindset. In most of the top ten states, for example (New York being the notable exception), aspiration and a commitment to institutional distinctiveness have yielded a leading national public university, plus a corresponding distinctiveness in other institutions. Contrary to popular opinion, this drive toward distinctiveness has not, for the most part, driven away minorities; rather, it has tended to keep in-state students at home. And all of this together has resulted in strong state funding support.

In conclusion, whether or not these ten states can boast the nation's best public university systems, they certainly rank among the best and thus provide a good standard for examination. Of course, impending changes ensure that even these "best" systems will face enormous challenges and, consequently, undergo their own metamorphoses during the next two decades. Yet, their excellent examples do promise insight for all aspiring states and institutions.

12

A Question of Leadership: American Higher Education as a Management Model

Despite serious problems and impending changes precipitated by the challenges of a new century, American colleges and universities represent an accumulated resource unparalleled in the world, an extremely valuable asset in the national quest for economic excellence.

Consider these facts: 3,200 American institutions of higher education enroll some 12 million students; over 95 percent of all Americans live within twenty to thirty minutes of a college or university; the 100 top research universities spend between $5 and $10 billion annually on basic and applied research; 1,000 community colleges are ideally situated in every niche of America to attack the problem of adult literacy and to train and retrain hundreds of thousands, possibly millions, of American workers each year; the location, admission policies, costs, and programs of the 3,200 institutions are varied enough to provide educational opportunities for all Americans, regardless of interest, ability, or means; and, finally, the faculty of these institutions, some 400,000 strong, represent a unique and immeasurable intellectual resource.

Beyond these educational and research contributions, however, America's colleges and universities offer the nation a further asset as a successful management model for the post-industrial age. The example of well-managed colleges and universities can provide insight into the administration of amorphous institutions in which the most highly paid workers are characterized by independence and a high level of education or training, i.e., the typical information age organization. This original American management design better suits the

132

requirements of American business than models from different cultures, including Japan, a recent source of inspiration for American business and industry in the quest for improved efficiency and productivity.

MANAGEMENT CHALLENGES OF A CHANGING WORK FORCE

Basic American management practices, shaped by the requirements of an industrial society, must be questioned and reevaluated in light of demands posed by a new and dramatically different postindustrial economy. A major challenge now facing American business and industry is learning how to manage a changing national work force—one more individualistic and highly educated, and charged with very different tasks than in the days of Henry Ford's automobile assembly line.

Yet current American (and European) management science and practice are largely based on the assembly line process, in which input is measured, everything is processed uniformly and serially, and output is measured for quality and efficiency. Hierarchical management structures, limited worker flexibility, cost accounting, efficiency studies, and other familiar components of the industrial economy grew from the assembly line's success. In this system, most workers possessed only limited education and training. They were expected to be highly proficient at a relatively simple task; they were not expected to be inventive. To a large extent, America's growth in productivity during the industrial golden age (roughly 1870 to 1950) can be attributed to continuous fine-tuning of Henry Ford's assembly line. But with Sputnik's 1957 flight into space, the seeds of a new economic order germinated, and a new age—both cultural and economic—began.

Today, in the 1990s, a maturing science- and technology-based economy, in which information has arguably become the most important commodity, is spawning dramatically different products and services. New materials have changed the way we cook our food, keep our records, write our letters and books, communicate with each other, travel locally or internationally, and, most importantly, do our work. In contrast to Henry Ford's era of factories and assembly line laborers, many of today's high-tech and service companies depend on a work force comprised of at least 70 percent professional employees. Further, American business and industry have already seen fundamental changes in the characteristics and training required of frontline workers. Unlike their predecessors, today's em-

ployees are extensively trained and/or educated; they are independent, critical, and outspoken; and, though they may perform a highly
specific job, they are often concerned with a wide range of a
company's functions. In fact, most companies now involve frontline
workers in product and process development and the decision-
making chain.

THE RELEVANCE OF UNIVERSITY MANAGEMENT

By no stretch of the imagination are all, or even most, of America's
colleges and universities suited to serve as management models for
industry. Nevertheless, many well-run colleges and universities provide excellent examples that can shed light on new business approaches to management. Institutions of higher education must
operate in a state of near-constant flux; they are staffed by independent and highly educated workers; and they function within the context of America's competing cultural forces. Because these
characteristics more closely parallel the emerging information age
organization than the traditional industrial age model, much can be
learned from the management successes of higher education institutions and their leaders.

The following exploration of management examples offered by
America's campuses resulted from twenty-five years of experience
and several research projects. The 1984 study of up-and-coming colleges and universities that led to the book *Searching for Academic
Excellence* also served as a primary resource here. Other material,
including studies of several high technology service companies in the
Washington, D.C. area, came from the George Mason University Center for Policy Studies in Education. In addition, this section includes
conclusions resulting from the author's observations during visits to
some 200 colleges and universities over a twenty-five-year period.

The findings based on this research are detailed in three sections,
focusing on the prototypical manager, exceptional higher education
leaders, and a selection of successful management principles.
Though it may seem these examples are targeted toward those at the
very top of the leadership hierarchy, they can be usefully applied by
men and women at a variety of management levels.

THE PROTOTYPICAL MANAGER

In examining the work of more than fifty highly successful college
and university leaders, five major leadership traits emerged that to-

gether define the prototypical manager. These five descriptive characterizations are: strategist, opportunist, team-builder, nurturer, and perspectivist.

George Johnson, president of George Mason University, has defined a *strategist* as a person who develops an eye for better surfboards and the perfect wave; by contrast, a bureaucrat attempts to build better seawalls. From another perspective, one might say the strategist pictures change as a central rather than peripheral force, while the bureaucrat views change as marginal or even threatening to an operation.

The *opportunist* is always looking for connections—connections between new ideas and organizational strengths and weaknesses. Like successful American industrialists Henry Ford and Thomas Edison, the opportunist knows that generating an original idea is not nearly as important as recognizing a good idea when it appears, and then figuring out how to use it.

The most important task of an opportunity-conscious leader is to seek out ideas and opportunities, then to sort, evaluate, and experiment. Though some individuals are better at this than others, such perception is an art that can be developed with practice. Looking for opportunities may mean regular and persistent attempts to "see over the horizon" or "around the bend" in an effort to anticipate future issues and possibilities. Or it may mean encouraging associates to generate ideas for improving processes or anticipating developments. Or it might include environmental scanning of competitors to identify strategies that could be adapted to one's own organization.

Developing a team feeling is another important trait of the prototypical manager. The *team-builder* realizes cooperation is vital in a knowledge-based enterprise. Synergy is crucial to the development of ideas; it fosters long-range views and broad perspective among employees; it builds loyalty through cooperative striving toward common goals; and it provides the disciplinary interaction essential for problem solving in a complex age. Teams are built on principles—dedication to an idea or project, matching complementary talents, or providing incentives to enhance the pursuit of common goals.

Nurturing, or encouraging individual initiative, is another critical component of organizational success. The *nurturer* plays an important role by stimulating the production of new ideas, new products, and new ways of doing things. Since the primary work force of the twenty-first century will be capable of making significant contributions to their companies—but only if properly motivated—nurturing holds significant promise for the future.

Finally, the prototypical manger is a *perspectivist*, one who finds ways to contribute to the community beyond his or her area of primary professional interest. It is all too easy in today's complex and stressful work environment for leaders to become immersed in the details of their work, a problem further complicated by the growing tendency toward specialization and the overwhelming quantity of detail to be mastered in every field.

Consequently, leaders must always strive for perspective: they must ensure that while looking at the trees (which may well be necessary), they don't overlook the forest. This does not mean, however, merely attending Rotary Club meetings, playing golf twice a week, or touring Europe; the point is not recreation or relaxation.

To strive for perspective is to become seriously involved in something of significance outside or paralleling one's primary work. This alternative life offers a fresh view of issues and people and can provide a new conceptual framework for detached consideration of professional problems.

CHALLENGES FACED BY LEADERS AND MANAGERS IN KNOWLEDGE INDUSTRIES

Examination of organizations effectively operating at the leading edge of the information age economy revealed the following leadership/management suggestions and challenges.

KEEP IN TOUCH WITH KEY WORKERS—THOSE PRODUCING THE PRODUCT OR INTERACTING WITH THE PRIMARY CUSTOMER. This may mean limiting activities that require extra staff and mid-management employees. In fact, management theorist Peter Drucker advocates major reductions: "Probably the greatest weakness in our big corporations is that they have built enormous hierarchies of management."[1]

The review of successful colleges and college presidents revealed a concern for channeling resources to those actually involved in teaching, research, and service—as opposed to mid-management staff. At Northeast Missouri State University, for example, President Charles McClain operated a 7,000-student institution with one-third the normal complement of top administrators—only one vice president, three deans, and eleven directors.

Keeping in touch with those on the firing line can also mean simply working and talking with people, finding out first hand what is going on. Listening is an important, yet often neglected, factor in communication, a lesson Japanese business people have learned better than Americans. In fact, one of the major observed differences between American and Japanese executives is that Americans seem compelled to talk, while the Japanese listen more carefully.

"The Achilles' heel of top management in the U.S. (is) they simply talk too darn much," commented Harvard Business School Professor D. Quinn Mills in June 1989.[2] "They talk to government officials, they talk to analysts, they give speech after speech to their own people, but overwhelmingly, they forget to listen."

DON'T BE TOTALLY COMMITTED TO CONSENSUS; FOCUS INSTEAD ON DEVELOPING THE BEST THINKING FROM TALENT WITHIN THE ORGANIZATION. "A camel is a horse designed by a committee," the old axiom declares, while a corollary jingle warns "A committee of one gets something done; a committee of twenty deliberates plenty." Of course, committees are useful, even essential, in most knowledge-based industries. They often serve an important role in shaping consensus. But too often committees become bureaucracies that choke out truly innovative thinking.

Successful managers find ways to organize and facilitate committee function. They realize the purpose and functions of committees should be clearly stated and bound by definite parameters at the outset. They are skillful in shopping for ideas and then, with the group's input, molding them into usability. Most importantly, successful managers know staying ahead of the curve in a time of rapid change demands full and open-minded maximization of the organization's best brains.

NO MATTER HOW LARGE, AN ORGANIZATION MUST BE MADE TO SEEM SMALL, BOTH TO EMPLOYEES AND TO CUSTOMERS. In an environment characterized by change and individualism, bigness or even the perception of bigness can adversely affect employee performance and customer service. Maintaining a personal touch, is both crucial and feasible, regardless of the organization's size.

A community college founded in the 1970s, for example, grew at the rate of 2,500 students per year for four years, becoming one of the largest colleges in the state. In spite of its huge size, however, students repeatedly spoke of the school as small and personal. To create this perception, the college had organized itself to conduct most staff/student contact functions in the academic divisions rather than at a central staff level. In fact, the central staff was small, virtually invisible, and dedicated primarily to planning and data collection functions.

ENCOURAGE PEOPLE TO ACT ENTREPRENEURIALLY WITHIN THE ORGANIZATION, REGARDLESS OF HOW LARGE IT IS. A plan of action to encourage entrepreneurial action should include:

- developing a clear statement of organizational direction—a plan as broad as the organization, but containing clear goals and a definite line of development;
- keeping a constant watch for people with ideas and the willingness to vigorously pursue them;
- focusing on responsibility, not bureaucratic process; rewarding people with good ideas without molding them into staff or bureaucrats;
- and encouraging all personnel to see risk-taking as better security than status in today's mutable environment.

BE A SPONSOR. Good managers identified in these studies invariably served as mentors, teaching other people and nurturing talent within the organization. More than just good business, helping another person grow professionally is personally rewarding. One manager interviewed took great pride in the number of people he had promoted to a first significant management job who had then gone on to become highly successful leaders themselves. In turn, this mentor reaped a business bonus. With such a track record, he found extraordinary numbers of energetic and capable young people attracted to his organization.

To be a successful mentor, a leader/manager must:

- always be on the lookout for creative people who work hard and get things done;
- see such people as an asset, not a threat; and
- give them encouragement, guidance, and recognition.

DEVELOP A SYSTEM FOR CHOOSING GOOD IDEAS. Too often, people in positions of responsibility rely on "seat of the pants" judgements, resulting in decisions often regretted later. Although some managers excel at this instinctive approach, most function more effectively with a rational decision-making process. In fact, even apparently intuitive decision-makers often follow an implicit set of principles. Regardless, with a little organization and practice, any person can improve his or her performance in evaluating ideas. Start with these characteristics of good ideas:

- Good ideas are usually simple, with a good measure of common sense.
- Good ideas address a real problem.
- As a corollary, because they address an understood problem, good ideas can be explained.
- To refine a good idea, consider and compare alternatives. Don't look for quick opportunities to shout an idea down;

there will be plenty of time for questions and criticism as an idea develops. And be sure to involve other people in exploring a good idea.

WORK AT ANTICIPATING IDEAS, TRENDS, AND CHANGES IN CONDITIONS AND MARKETS. Very few people actually have the foresight to predict the future; however, people who know how to identify trends are positioned to take advantage of change. By thinking about changes in their organization's operational environment, certain leaders are able to identify opportunities earlier than others. Perhaps even more important, an organization that works to anticipate change perceives the exploitation of change as critical to future growth and development—an attitude that encourages entrepreneurial rather than bureaucratic thinking.

CONCLUSION

Though the American higher education system faces problems, and America's business leaders seem preoccupied with Japanese management and education models, the world continues to look to America for excellence in higher education.

For players in the developing science- and knowledge-based economy of the next century, American higher education represents an enormous resource. American colleges and universities can generate new knowledge, turn out first-rate graduates, provide excellent continuing education opportunities, and help identify and produce new products. Further, America's colleges and universities can strengthen the drive toward increased national competitiveness by offering an instructive management model for American business and industry.

Not all universities, maybe not even a majority, are well-managed, but higher education can offer a valuable service by sharing the lessons of its hundred-year struggle to manage organizations that do not conform to industrial models. Perhaps inevitably, the workplace of the post-industrial economy is looking more and more like that of the university environment—highly trained frontline workers operating in a multicultural, heterogeneous environment. For these reasons, valuable management lessons can be learned from this nation's best run universities, lessons rooted in the cultural experience of America. We need not travel to the Orient for hints in management excellence; we can simply step onto campus, right next door.

13

Coordinating Boards and the Politicization of American Higher Education

> We have a six-year program planning cycle, tied to the biennial budget process and the state's six-year capital outlay planning system. Therefore, it would be virtually impossible to approve a new program in the summer of 1989 for implementation in either 1990 or 1991. We could consider this program for the 1992–94 cycle.

This was the response of a state higher education coordinating board when one of its universities asked permission to start a new undergraduate degree program. No one questioned that the proposed program was urgently needed, nor did money pose a problem, thanks to a five million dollar pledge of private funds for scholarship and program development. The board's staff response, as characterized by a faculty member, communicated their inflexible stance: "We can't put round pegs in square holes except on odd years in a six-year cycle!" In other words, for these bureau staff, nothing outweighed the importance of process and regulation.

Ironically, this incident followed the release of a two-year study of that state's higher education system, particularly its readiness to serve in the twenty-first century. A blue ribbon panel spoke powerfully in their report of impending changes precipitated by the emergence of new world forces, a new economy, and a new century. It focused on the subsequent need to do things differently, to be more flexible. But the benefits of flexibility were obviously lost on central staff members who stubbornly defended the inviolate nature of six-year plans.

FROM REGULATION TO DEREGULATION

Even as these state staff deliberated, the Soviet Empire began to crumble, and socialism waned around the globe. In all the world, there was no more obvious a failure than the Soviets' centrally-imposed five-year plan. Not only in communist nations, but also in world capitals from London to Tokyo to Washington, D.C., central planning and regulation began yielding to deregulation and individual incentive.

One result of Washington's recent bent toward deregulation has been an increased expectation for states to assume additional responsibility in many areas, including higher education. Reacting to this partial withdrawal of federal support, many young, ambitious, and well-educated governors of the 1980s, recognizing the importance of higher education to their states, seized the opportunity to establish state direction of colleges and universities.

By contrast, higher education state staffs spoke little in the early 1980s of flexibility, decentralization, or the relationship between higher education and the economy. In fact, even to date, most of this talk has originated with governors, institutions, and private sector corporations and foundations.

Consequently, when these aggressive governors turned their attention to higher education, many were disturbed to find what seemed to be just another "special interest" group, eager for more state money, but, at the same time, rigid and unresponsive to the needs of the nation. (See chapter 9.) In most cases, reform-minded governors discovered a largely inflexible system, one created to "control growth, avoid unnecessary duplication, and provide accountability." Additional state higher education goals—"to promote accessibility and ensure quality"—had often resulted in a complex, unbending maze of regulations.

The pressure that came to bear on higher education during the 1980s from governors, legislators, and the private sector resulted in struggling institutions and increasingly bureaucratic state staffs. Another outcome was the increased politicization of state higher education systems as political leaders, rightly or wrongly, sought to make systems more responsive.

INCREASED POLITICAL INFLUENCE

Governors and legislators have become irritated with inflexible and unresponsive higher education systems, and with cause. One casualty of this reaction has been the tradition of appointing scholars to head university systems. Nationwide, departing system heads have increasingly been replaced by politicians and/or business people. In North Carolina, for instance, legendary UNC President William Friday was succeeded by C. D. Spangler, a Charlotte contractor who served on the State Board of Education, a body that governs public schools, not colleges. And former governor Robert Scott is president of that state's community college system. In Tennessee, former governor Lamar Alexander and former state senator Thomas Garland serve as top system administrators. In Florida and Oklahoma, the current system heads were previously executive assistants to governors. And in Oregon and Maryland, top higher education officials are political appointees of Governors Goldschmidt and Schaefer.

By contrast, executive directors of state coordination boards tend to lack experience in higher education, politics, and business. (One notable exception is Dr. Charles McClain, the highly successful president of Northeast Missouri State University, who retired to become Missouri's Commissioner of Higher Education.) Typically these people come from a close circle of State Higher Education Executive Officers (SHEEO) staffers. The current head of the Minnesota coordinating board, for example, served as the chief deputy at the now defunct West Virginia Board of Regents, while the recently appointed head of the New Mexico coordinating board was formerly the second in command in Minnesota.

THE BEST STATE RESPONSE: NEW JERSEY

Perhaps the best and most successful example of state intervention to create a more responsive and better higher education system can be found in New Jersey. There, during the mid-1980s, former Governor Thomas Kean set in motion dual forces for change: deregulation and incentives.

Prior to Kean's action, New Jersey operated one of the most overregulated systems of higher education in the nation. Despite expansion and creation of new institutions since World War II, the New Jersey system remained largely undistinguished. But Kean's move to deregulate is promoting a new spirit of enthusiasm among the state's public colleges and universities.

Kean's second tactic—offering financial incentives in response to solicited proposals for change by college administrators—provided the catalyst to effect major changes. Institutions submitting well-developed strategies were rewarded with state-funded challenge grants approaching eight figures—enough real money to provide significant incentive to change. And in New Jersey, change is evident.

CALCIFIED STATE AGENCIES

Attempting to hold their ground against the shifting sands of inevitable change, state higher education agencies have sometimes taken positions which made them appear ridiculous and counterproductive. In one western state with upper division universities, the coordination agency has acted aggressively to prevent these schools from becoming "full four year" institutions. One institution, for example, an upper division, graduate university, was encouraged by the state agency to create a comprehensive Japan study center. But the agency later vetoed the university's plan to offer noncredit, conversational Japanese to the center's supporters in the business community. The agency's rationale was that an upper division university could not offer beginning languages. That was the job of area community colleges and other public and private baccalaureate institutions. It didn't matter that the proposed course required no state funding and in no way resembled a standard foreign language course. The agency stood firm, so committed to non-duplication as to be calcified in its position.

Fallout from the agency's decision was so furious that the state legislature passed a bill changing the university to a full four-year university. Had the agency been responsive and encouraging rather than dictatorial and inflexible, the entire unpleasant incident could have been avoided. This university could have served its constituency, and the agency could have maintained its control over "unnecessary duplication."

The goal of non-duplication all too frequently becomes an end in itself, leading to jury-rigged attempts to mandate institutional cooperation. In the mid–1980s, for example, three neighboring institutions—the University of Maryland, Morgan State University, and Towson State University—proposed a truly cooperative degree program in foreign languages so competitive it required students to take at least six credit hours at each of the three colleges. Though painstakingly developed over a period of three years, the proposal was returned to the institutions by the Maryland Higher Education Board (later abolished by Governor Schaefer), along with the suggestion that all three institutions should be named on each diploma to further ensure cooperation and thus avoid unnecessary duplication! This type of obsessive inflexibility discourages institutions from cooperation, as well as innovation.

In another example of agency calcification in the matter of non-duplication, the State Council for Higher Education in Virginia tried to scuttle a 1985 proposal by the George Mason University School of Nursing to establish an innovative new doctoral program. At that time, the state offered one nursing doctorate (at the University of Virginia), which had not proven as successful as expected when approved by the Council over a competing proposal by the Medical College of Virginia in Richmond.

In an effort to create additional competition, the Council staff delayed its decision on the George Mason proposal while quietly sharing the plan with the Medical College of Virginia and asking for a competing proposal. In due course, two proposals came before the Council, along with staff recommendations to approve the MCV proposal and reject the GMU plan. The decision was further delayed, however, when the Council's vice-chair requested—and won—an outside review of the two programs.

To the surprise of virtually everyone, the reviewers (prominent nursing deans from out-of-state) recommended approval of both programs, or—if the state could approve only one—the George Mason plan alone. The reviewers praised the George Mason nursing faculty as among the best in the nation, noting that it ranked fourth nationwide in the number of doctoral faculty.

To make a long story short, Virginia now offers three doctoral programs in nursing rather than one or even two. The George Mason program, so nearly vetoed by the Council, is thriving and attracting national attention. Its example again illustrates the folly of ignoring merit and innovation in blind pursuit of non-duplication.

SUMMARY AND RECOMMENDATIONS

Clearly, America's institutions require both flexibility and incentives to effect the changes necessary to meet the demands of the twenty first century. Yet, state higher education coordinating boards are not voluntarily becoming more flexible. Possibly, this entrenched stance stems from the limited authority accorded to coordinating boards, which fosters a tendency toward posturing and regulation in order to create the appearance of real authority. In some cases, however, these boards are doubtlessly motivated by a genuine desire to better the higher education systems they govern.

The recent trend toward appointing politicians and/or business people to top administrative positions within university systems represents one attempt to sidestep the bureaucratic morass. Such appointments can be a good move if these system heads act with common sense and integrity, and win the confidence of governors and legislators.

The example of New Jersey's Thomas Kean indicates that direct interaction by a governor in setting goals for higher education, if handled correctly, can also prove productive in achieving constructive change. But state governing boards must not continue to stand in the way of higher education's evolution. The pressure to implement new ideas will only increase in the decade ahead; institutions and their leaders must be free to boldly meet the challenge of accelerating change.

14

Academic Strategy: Advice for Multicampus Governing Boards

Try to imagine how things might change during the 1990s as America and the world approach a new century, a new millennium, a new economic age. The prospects are as staggering as they are unknown. Political events in eastern Europe during 1989 and 1990, for example, unfolded at a dazzling pace. One by one, infant democracies sprouted and took hold, rising quickly above the ashes of communism. Who would have thought economics and a few ideas could turn the world upside down, virtually overnight? Contrary to George Orwell's forecast, the information/electronic age has abolished rather than institutionalized thought control. Ideas are powerful!

Undoubtedly, the decade of the 1990s will continue to yield dramatic, unpredictable change. The world is growing smaller, international economics are unstable, and the United States is challenged to remain competitive. We must fundamentally rethink ideas and principles once thought settled. In this age of fluctuating international economics, however, one thing is certain. Education is the crucial ingredient necessary to ensure a productive and competitive America in the twenty-first century. As American higher education looks toward a fluid future, impending changes guarantee dramatic implications for effective planning, especially for governing boards with multiple campuses. The educational leadership now in place, including these boards of control, bears an enormous responsibility for the future.

Though higher education and public schools in the United States are positioned differently to meet the new era, both face major challenges demanding astute leadership. By most measures and almost any report, America's public schools are in trouble. Despite a decade of talk, action, and spending on school reform, no real progress is discernible. The United States cannot be called an educational leader by any international standard. Without question, fundamental revolution, not patchwork methodology, is required—and now!

America's colleges and universities face different but equally formidable challenges. Though one of the few United States products still in great worldwide demand, American higher education must overcome serious obstacles. For example:

- American colleges and universities are admonished to constantly improve their quality and accessibility—without expecting more financing. The American public is railing at higher education for hiking its prices, yet, at the same time, education is slipping as a priority for public funds.
- Current faculty members are aging, but academically oriented youngsters who might replace them are drawn toward more lucrative professions. It is a certainty, therefore, that American colleges will face a shortage of quality faculty in the late 1990s. Though earning a Ph.D. degree in physics, biology, or chemistry requires as challenging and lengthy a process as becoming a medical doctor, and the doctorate in social sciences or humanities is at least as difficult to achieve as a law degree or an MBA, an academic career seldom offers the same financial rewards as these other professions. Consequently, talent sorely needed to maintain an excellent, competitive college and university system is being siphoned off into other professional arenas.
- Colleges and universities must be global in their thinking, technological in practice, entrepreneurial in nature, and responsive to both change and public demand. At the same time, however, they must be more accountable to bureaus and legislators. The focus on eliminating "unnecessary duplication," in particular, still fuels hot debate in many states.
- With the collapse of the Soviet empire and socialism, it seems strange that American higher education alone still maintains faith in "five-year plans." Considering the dramatic changes and challenges facing American colleges and universities, planning must be flexible and proactive! This need for effective planning is perhaps the fundamental challenge facing American higher education.

To plan adequately in a time of uncertainty and great expectations, governing boards with multicampus responsibilities are increasingly challenged to manage and position their institutions in order to exploit change rather than fear it. All too frequently, however, the response is a bureaucratic, linear planning process based on the assumption that the immediate and even the long-range future will resemble the immediate past. Should not planning for the 1990s originate instead from experimental, entrepreneurial guidance? The planning goal should be to encourage and assist institutions within a system as they position themselves to maximize the opportunities certain to develop. In uncertain times, times of transition, opportunities will occur at regular frequencies. Those positioned to take advantage of these occasions will be the successful, model institutions of the twenty-first century.

Some guidance for those who would position their institutions to exploit change can be found in recent experiences and research. The concept of academic strategy, for example, a movement fathered in large part by Richard Cyert and George Keller, is a useful approach. A recent derivation of academic strategy—*referenced as selective excellence*—has found success in a wide range of American institutions of higher education. Another source of ideas is the book *Higher Education and the Public Trust*. To build institutional stature, this text proposes, planning should focus on the point where institutional strengths and interests intersect with the public interest.[1] Finally, there are numerous examples of individual institutions across the country that built stature during the 1980s through the use of academic strategy. These schools include Carnegie Mellon, George Mason, Northeast Missouri, and Bradford College, among many others.

It is possible for multicampus governing boards to bring these theories and principles together to shape a coherent theory of strategic management. This approach to facing future challenges and institution building includes the following steps: developing a system context statement; building individual institutional strategies focused on distinction within and without a state; ensuring that these strategies are aspirational in nature; and displaying an emphasis on cooperative, intra-institutional planning, i.e., tying the system together by strengthening its programs in a cost-effective way. The following sections describe this approach to planning.

• First, the governing board should develop a *context statement* at the system level to provide institutional planning guidance. This statement focuses primarily on the major social and governmental issues—both national and state—facing the institution and its constituency. For example, a context statement for a particular state system might specifically reference such issues as competitiveness and economic development, improvement of public schools, and participation of minorities in higher education and in a competitive economy. Other issues might include poverty, leadership, or the environment, among others.

- Next, each institution within the system should develop its own strategy for the future, focusing on the distinctiveness of the campus, both within the state and nationally. This strategy should also take into account tradition, strengths, location, and opportunities. Development of an academic strategy for a particular campus should include significant work at the grassroots level. (Cyert, for example, began his strategic planning at Carnegie Mellon in 1972 by asking individual academic departments how the university could be distinctive.) Individual campuses must be held accountable to the context statement and, in most cases, focus on doing a limited number of things well (the selected excellence approach). It is important during this development phase to ensure an open process by communicating with other system campuses, external constituents, and the general public.

- As the work toward an academic strategy proceeds on each campus, it should be monitored by the system governing board in case the need arises for adjustments to the context statement. Since the system context must be a shared vision, institutional input and the ability for flexible revision are critical to the success of this approach. System-wide coordination is also important.

- Finally, the governing board must look beyond the context statement for additional ways to knit the entire system together and answer cost-effectiveness questions. For example, it may seem to be expensive, unnecessary duplication for a three-campus system to offer three MBA programs, but not politically feasible to eliminate any one of them. (A surprising number of smaller systems offer similar MBA degrees at every institution. Other degrees with the same duplicating potential include education, engineering, and occasionally medicine or law.)

To defuse these touchy situations, a board can insist that each campus develop its own distinctive strategy by referencing the others. One campus could build strength in an appropriate area and then share that with the other system campuses. (Sharing can take many forms, such as visiting or exchange professors, special institutes, or the use of interactive television.) Specific strengths might include economics, international business, or the use of technology in business. This example is not to imply that only one institution should teach a certain subject, economics, for instance, but rather that only one would strive to make economics the lead discipline in its business program and then share this strength with other campuses. In such a strategy, the question of duplication is addressed proactively and in a way that builds an entirely new level of quality for the state while effectively tying the system together.

A system strategy that focuses on distinctiveness through the emphasis of different programs at different campuses, that addresses the state's greatest concerns through a carefully crafted context statement, and that commits to building quality into the planning process provides the best framework for developing a proactive, twenty-first-century-oriented system of colleges. Such a strategy also carries the enormous advantage of addressing the cost-effectiveness question—an imperative in a nation growing short of resources.

There is no question that change will continue, change that will be difficult, if not impossible, to predict. "Business as usual" will simply not work as an effective leadership position in the 1990s. This change represents a major challenge to governing boards in multi-campus systems. How effective these boards are in planning for change will determine whether they will represent the future—or the past! Some will prosper in the 1990s while others falter. Only time will determine which systems fall into which category.

PART THREE

New Challenges and New Universities

America's initial entries into the knowledge age of the future can be traced to certain metropolitan areas throughout the country where technology and information first combined on a large scale. The results eventually caused a shift of economic preeminence from aging industrial centers to progressive urban regions such as Atlanta, southern California, central Florida, northern Virginia, and central Maryland. These thriving areas provided a catalytic environment for the emergence of a new, science-driven society. Characterized primarily by rapid and dramatic expansion, America's hypergrowth regions are now leading the nation toward a new century dominated by ideas and technology.

The impact of emerging regional economies will transform institutions of higher education located in burgeoning metropolitan areas. New educational strategies, approaches and structures must be quickly assembled to meet the voracious information appetite of a knowledge-based society. The response of frontline institutions located in hypergrowth areas offers insight into factors affecting the future shape and attitude of all colleges and universities.

Even now, sparsely populated rural areas can benefit from the lessons of the urban environment. Institutions in both settings are moving to integrate technology into the education process as a means of reaching widely distributed populations. The heightened value of education in a world based on knowledge demands that colleges and universities deliver relevant, high-quality educational services, accessible to all Americans.

The final section of the book explores these new challenges facing higher education. In chapter 15, Dr. Edward Delaney and Dr. Donald Norris report the results of their extensive research on the higher education needs of hypergrowth regions and the responses of both individual institutions and academic consortia. Chapter 16 continues this discussion, focusing on the concept of the distributed university as a means of disseminating educational services through the use of technology and innovative academic organizations. Finally, Chapter 17 summarizes the conclusions and recommendations of previous chapters for the convenience of readers who may want to refer back to various ideas presented in this book.

15

New Ways of Serving Hypergrowth Regions

EDWARD L. DELANEY AND DONALD M. NORRIS

Many of the nation's metropolitan areas are currently undergoing a series of highly significant economic, demographic, and social changes that are affecting the ways in which people live, work, and learn. The new and expanded educational programs and initiatives of colleges and universities in these metropolitan areas suggest the birth of new educational models of instructional, research, and service delivery.

A NEW PATTERN OF URBAN DEVELOPMENT

Beginning in the 1970s, and increasingly in the 1980s, metropolitan areas in the United States changed both quantitatively and qualitatively. The 1990 United States Census will likely document the full extent of this growth, which is altering the balance of economic, social, and political power in many states. A forward scan into the 1990s suggests these developments will continue and may even accelerate. By the year 2000, a new type of metropolitan area will likely change the nation's domestic service needs, including educational requirements. This emergent form of metropolitan development has been described as a new, interconnected network of urban villages or satellite cities.

The former industrial model for urban growth and development began with a highly developed urban core, surrounded by concentric circles of decreasing development, as mitigated by natural geographic and social barriers. Though an urban core may experience cycles of decay and regeneration over time, the concentric circle model guided generations of city planners and urbanologists who saw the city as the hub of commerce, culture, and education.

By the 1980s, however, it became clear that metropolitan areas were no longer growing in the classic manner. Instead, new centers of development began emerging in strings or circles around center cities, following the systems of freeways and major highways. Originally intended as transportation bypasses to expedite interstate traffic around urban centers, freeways and beltways have become the foundation for suburban downtowns and satellite cities.

Often centered around a large, regional shopping mall, these nodes of development have become major centers of employment. They include medium-height office buildings and other commercial facilities, plus acres of parking lots and structures. Moreover, people are living within close proximity of these emerging urban villages and, where possible, seeking their recreation and cultural diversions near their homes in these suburban downtowns rather than venturing into the central city.

In the United States, several metropolitan areas exhibit the urban villages configuration, particularly outlying counties around New York, Washington, Atlanta, Los Angeles, San Diego, San Francisco, Seattle, Tampa, Miami, Dallas, Houston, St. Louis, Minneapolis, and Chicago. Cities in many foreign nations in Europe, South America, and Asia are experiencing similar trends, suggesting that the urban village is emerging as an international phenomenon.

FORCES SHAPING EDUCATIONAL POTENTIALS
IN METROPOLITAN AREAS

The development of urban villages has become a dominant force in shaping metropolitan areas, as well as the leading factor in the creation of unique new educational potentials in these areas. This phenomenon, together with other forces, offers unique challenges and opportunities for higher education. Figure 15.1 outlines these factors, which are discussed below.

DEVELOPMENT OF URBAN VILLAGES. As centers of high-tech employment, growing urban villages are altering demographic and political balances of power in many states and regions. Following the political

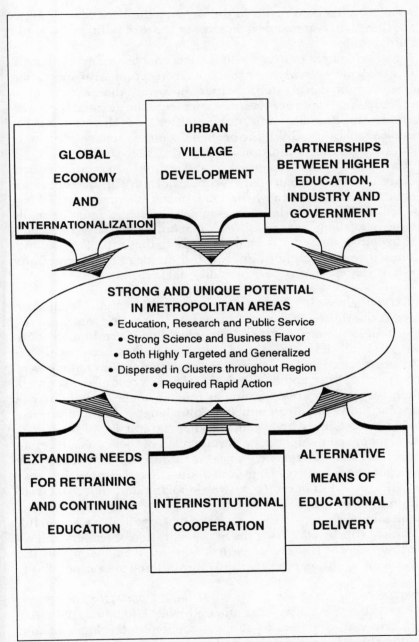

FIGURE 15.1. Forces Shaping Educational Potentials in Metropolitan Areas

redistribution likely to result in the wake of the 1990 census, areas such as these will command an increasing share of political power in the United States.

The development of urban villages has enabled many metropolitan areas to grow even in the absence of strong public transportation systems. Within these satellite cities, however, the service infrastructure has not kept pace with development. The demand for transportation, public services, cultural activities, and education has far exceeded availability. Given the probable continued pace of growth, planners are seeking new means of delivering such services.

Development has also served to cluster and regionalize educational needs in these urban areas. As potential students become more placebound because of the urban clustering phenomenon, educational, cultural, and personal development offerings must be made available near their homes and work-places. Higher education's capacity to deliver new educational offerings to these students, including the nature of disciplines offered and the degree of community support, is shaped by a variety of additional factors.

THE GLOBAL ECONOMY AND INTERNATIONALIZATION. As detailed in chapter 7, the United States is confronting increasing international competition in science, business, and education. Certain metropolitan areas on the East, West, and Gulf coasts that serve as portal points for international activities are experiencing the challenges of international culture and business ahead of the rest of the country. Further, these areas are emerging as models of the new industrial pattern for the 1990s: clean industry, knowledge-based and service-based economies, and a highly entrepreneurial spirit.

As planners contemplate the development of these coastal urban villages, it is clear that they will serve as gateways to global economics, science, and culture. High-tech industries clustered in these urban villages are inherently outward-looking and more likely to maintain a global focus.

Educational centers in these growing metropolitan areas can fulfill a critical role by educating the next generation of leaders and rededicating current leaders, scientists, and business people to the importance of global perspective and international operations skills.

STRENGTHENING PARTNERSHIPS AMONG HIGHER EDUCATION, INDUSTRY, AND GOVERNMENT. Partnerships among higher education, industry, and government, designed to support economic development and technology transfer, are gaining in strength and sophistication. The greatest opportunities for such partnerships are present in the hypergrowth metropolitan areas, and in their emergent satellite cities. To best avail themselves of these opportunities, some universities are clustering their educational and research resources near industrial partners, while others are encouraging industry to locate close to their campuses.

At the same time, even public universities are developing greater sophistication in joint development ventures with private-sector partners, as reflected in research parks, incubators, and new campuses. California State University-Northridge, for example, is developing a $250 million joint development of academic, residential, research, commercial and recreational facilities through a public/private development partnership, without state fiscal support. Clearly, joint ventures of this kind are most feasible in metropolitan areas, where the opportunities for multiple use are greatest.

Because many developing metropolitan areas differ politically or culturally from the mainstream in their state, response time to educational needs in these areas is often slowed. As a result, partnerships among industry, education and government in these areas have been important in overcoming opposition and accelerating the pace of educational development.

EXPANDING NEEDS FOR RETRAINING AND CONTINUING EDUCATION. The emerging information-based economy requires opportunities for significant retraining and continuing education to meet the employment and development needs of a sophisticated and educated work force, particularly in metropolitan areas. Changing patterns of education and work require that highly educated persons be able to seek degrees, credit learning, or noncredit learning to help improve their employment position, seek new careers, or launch entrepreneurial ventures.

Many continuing education needs in urban areas focus on the widening gulf between increasing skill requirements of manufacturing and technical employment in the 1990s and the decreasing capabilities of many graduates of inner city and even metropolitan school districts. If the United States is to be competitive in the global economy of the 1990s, it must address this problem. Solutions must be discovered in the metropolitan areas, in partnerships between local government, local universities, and business. Thus, the metropolitan area and its urban villages are becoming an essential laboratory for solving a variety of educational problems, at both the postsecondary and K–12 levels.

INTERINSTITUTIONAL COOPERATION. As public universities become more entrepreneurial, the once firm distinctions between public and private institutions have blurred, resulting in enhanced potential for cooperative ventures. Many metropolitan areas are served by a number of institutions, located both within and outside the region. But even these consortia are often inadequate to serve the escalating level of need.

Increasingly, institutions in remote locations find themselves in a highly disadvantaged position in competing for scientific and corporate resources clustered in urban centers. Consequently, greater cooperation and collaboration is occurring between urban universities and those that offer specialized programs, but are located outside the metropolitan region.

Because a single institution cannot typically generate sufficient resources to address the full range of programs and course offerings required in emerging metropolitan areas, interest is growing in inter-institutional cooperation, and in new organizational arrangements and other creative mechanisms designed to concentrate educational resources in these areas.

ALTERNATE MEANS OF EDUCATIONAL DELIVERY. In the emergent information age, educators are searching for alternate means of educational delivery through telecommunications, video, and other media, both to serve remote locations and to enhance traditional instruction in urban areas. Together with accelerating improvements in the instructional use of microprocessors, telecommunications technology offers new and promising tools for delivering educational services in urban village centers.

These advances in instructional delivery will likely foster new models for metropolitan education. By providing new means of instruction in multiple locations, technological approaches to education can become the glue that binds together the numerous learning sites required in urban areas. Further, these new technologies are encouraging educators to reexamine and change age-old teaching techniques. This process of change is likely to alter substantially the instructional methods employed in most academic disciplines, especially in metropolitan areas.

UNIQUE EDUCATIONAL OPPORTUNITIES IN METROPOLITAN AREAS

At least five major forces are shaping a variety of promising and unique educational opportunities in metropolitan areas.

THE REQUIREMENTS OF EDUCATION, RESEARCH, AND PUBLIC SERVICE MUST ALL BE SERVED IN METROPOLITAN AREAS. The needs of emerging urban villages are not limited to education alone, but include a full range of research and public service requirements as well. These urban areas thus challenge educators to deliver a balanced mixture of education, research, and public service activities.

THE NEEDS OF THESE METROPOLITAN REGIONS INCLUDE A STRONG SCIENCE AND BUSINESS THEME. The greatest potential for educational service to urban villages focuses on academic disciplines and partnership activities with a strong links to science and technology. High-level business and professional education areas are also in great demand.

EDUCATIONAL NEEDS ARE BOTH HIGHLY TARGETED AND GENERALIZED. Though the strongest educational needs of metropolitan areas involve science, business, and professional disciplines, urban villages also present broad, generalized needs for continuing learning and basic education in a wide range of academic disciplines at all levels from the associate degree through doctoral study. Many of these generalized needs, however, involve new disciplines or skills rather than traditional academic disciplines. New multidisciplinary academic approaches are necessary to meet these needs.

EDUCATIONAL NEEDS TEND TO BE DISPERSED IN CLUSTERS THROUGHOUT THE METROPOLITAN REGION. Urban villages can become focal points for serving the widespread educational needs of a metropolitan region. To effectively serve these urban villages, however, educators must understand their dynamics as centers of work, residence, and learning.

EDUCATION, RESEARCH, AND PUBLIC SERVICE NEEDS IN METROPOLITAN AREAS REQUIRE RAPID RESPONSE. Urban villages are characterized by hypergrowth, resulting in exploding economic development and the need for rapid technology transfer. They are neither able nor willing to tolerate the extended lead time for planning and approval of new educational offerings so typical of the education establishment. Instead, these urban growth areas demand accelerated development of high quality education, research, and public service programs.

TAILORING METROPOLITAN UNIVERSITIES
TO MEET THESE NEEDS

In response to these demands and opportunities, a number of new institutions, branch campuses, and other educational models are developing in the nation's fastest growing metropolitan areas. Even those institutions that have chosen traditional organizational structures have tailored their offerings to meet the needs of these urban villages. The following list summarizes several aspects of these new educational models.

- Programmatic Focus and Theming
- New Organizational and Administrative Structures
- New Staffing Patterns
- New Uses of Technology
- Strong Community Involvement
- Public/Private Partnerships and New Sources of Funding
- Enhanced Interinstitutional Cooperation
- Cultural and Quality of Life Components
- Accelerated Development

PROGRAMS ARE FOCUSED AND "THEMED." Some of the new educational initiatives attempt to offer a broad range of academic disciplines, and many of them are highly traditional in approach. Most, however, in some way recognize the need to focus and "theme" their programs based on characteristics of the metropolitan area they serve. Some new educational centers are highly targeted to the economic development and technology transfer requirements of their particular region.

NEW ORGANIZATIONAL AND ADMINISTRATIVE STRUCTURES ARE ATTRACTIVE IN SOME METROPOLITAN SETTINGS. In many metropolitan areas, traditional branch campus and extension center models have been used to deliver expanded offerings. But in some areas, especially those attempting to expand opportunities for collaboration by a number of institutions, new types of institutional forms and models are emerging. These innovative models include university centers, targeted high-tech institutes, and distributed universities.

NEW APPROACHES TO STAFFING ARE IMPORTANT. Science and business, the predominant academic disciplines of many metropolitan educational centers, are frequently the disciplines most affected by faculty shortages. To overcome these shortages and find new ways of providing instruction and developing multidisciplinary clusters, some institutions are experimenting with non-tenure-track appointments and creative employment of experienced professionals.

NEW USES OF TECHNOLOGY ARE IMPORTANT. Telecommunications and microprocessors have become important components of education, particularly in many of the emerging urban centers. Indeed, their use is expected by sophisticated learners and necessary in decentralized settings. Other operations, including administrative transactions, library information retrieval, and student record access, also rely extensively on avant garde developments in information technology.

STRONG COMMUNITY INVOLVEMENT IS CRITICAL TO THE METROPOLITAN UNIVERSITY. In almost all emerging metropolitan areas, local business and government leaders have provided critical intervention, funding, and political support to help launch a community-based educational presence.

PUBLIC/PRIVATE PARTNERSHIPS AND NEW SOURCES OF FUNDING ARE ESSENTIAL. In addition to strong community involvement, many new urban educational centers have utilized public-private partnerships and creative funding sources to cut through the Gordian knot of state funding and launch initiatives on an accelerated schedule. These partnerships and new funding sources are critical in expanding both the political support and programmatic focus of these educational ventures.

ENHANCED INSTITUTIONAL COOPERATION. Many urban village educational centers involve the participation of more than one institution of higher education. Effective articulation, cooperative program development, and institutional differentiation between community colleges and universities are fundamental in the metropolitan setting. Some models call for strong cooperation between institutions, while others couple institutions less tightly. Clearly, however, the higher educational needs of developing metropolitan areas are diverse, requiring the resources of a variety of institutions.

CULTURAL AND QUALITY OF LIFE COMPONENTS. Among the most critical components of urban village educational centers are programs that deal with cultural and quality-of-life concerns of area residents. The Japanese have found that lack of attention to these needs results in sterile living and learning clusters. In this area, metropolitan universities can play a vital role in developing urban village life.

ACCELERATED DEVELOPMENT. Many new metropolitan educational initiatives have experienced an accelerated rate of development compared to institutions in more traditional settings. Whether through creative financial arrangements, strong community involvement, or new organizational approaches, the new educational models are shortening the time traditionally required to establish new educational initiatives.

THE INSTITUTIONAL RESPONSE: NEW CAMPUSES AND NEW TYPES OF CAMPUSES

The emergence of urban villages with their related forces has accelerated the development of educational initiatives in rapidly growing metropolitan areas. In many cases, the response has been to utilize existing institutions or to establish new branches of existing institutions, to deliver traditional offerings. In more recent developments, however, the special needs of urban villages are being addressed by new organizational forms, and/or new and creative means of instructional delivery. (Figure 15.2 illustrates the educational models evolving in hypergrowth metropolitan areas.)

BRANCH CAMPUSES. A traditional way of establishing a new campus in a growing area has been to form a branch campus or extension center of an existing institution. In some cases, the branch remains part of a single institution. The University of Michigan, University of South Florida, and University of Minnesota are examples of branch or coordinated campuses that have followed this pattern.

In other states, branch campuses have been established with the expectation that if they grew to sufficient critical mass, they would ultimately become independent institutions. For example, three new campuses of the California State University System—San Marcos, Ventura, and Contra Mesa—recently opened as branches, with the prospect of ultimately becoming autonomous institutions.

The traditional branch campus model is a single campus presence serving a single community, often at a distance from the mother campus. But not all urban villages, many of which are located ten to twenty traffic-congested miles from the mother institution, are likely to offer the critical mass necessary to support a traditional branch campus. Moreover, the educational needs of these metropolitan areas are focused in business, science, engineering, and the performing arts—often at the graduate level. The traditional, full-service branch campus is seldom feasible or appropriate in these circumstances. Consequently, some institutions are experimenting with new approaches in establishing branch campuses. In Phoenix, for example, Arizona State University has recently established its West Campus as an upper level and graduate branch.

Even metropolitan campuses that have taken a traditional organizational tack have demonstrated creativity in responding to metropolitan needs. California State University-Northridge, an institution of 30,000 students in the San Fernando Valley, is using private funds to develop its "University Park" campus on 100 acres of land adjacent to the mother campus. Portions of the property will be used for

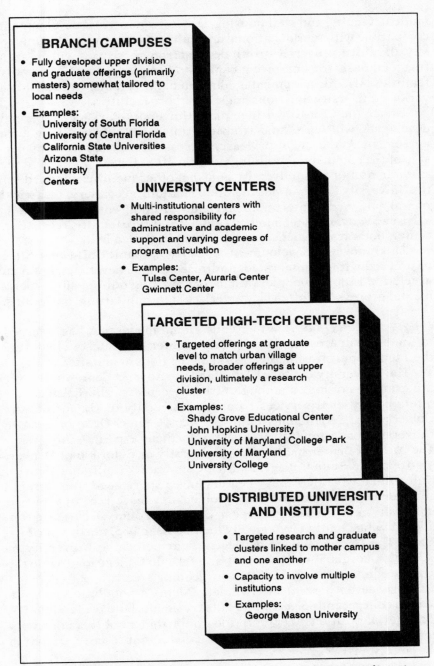

BRANCH CAMPUSES

- Fully developed upper division and graduate offerings (primarily masters) somewhat tailored to local needs
- Examples:
  University of South Florida
  University of Central Florida
  California State Universities
  Arizona State University Centers

UNIVERSITY CENTERS

- Multi-institutional centers with shared responsibility for administrative and academic support and varying degrees of program articulation
- Examples:
  Tulsa Center, Auraria Center
  Gwinnett Center

TARGETED HIGH-TECH CENTERS

- Targeted offerings at graduate level to match urban village needs, broader offerings at upper division, ultimately a research cluster
- Examples:
  Shady Grove Educational Center
  John Hopkins University
  University of Maryland College Park
  University of Maryland University College

DISTRIBUTED UNIVERSITY AND INSTITUTES

- Targeted research and graduate clusters linked to mother campus and one another
- Capacity to involve multiple institutions
- Examples:
  George Mason University

FIGURE 15.2. Models for Educational Institutions in Metropolitan Areas

student, faculty, and staff housing, and for commercial development compatible with the educational and cultural purposes of the university. In return, university profit derived from these uses will create a financial basis for borrowing capital to build additional university facilities. After development is completed, the revenue will subsidize various university functions housed in those facilities.

Under the CSU-Northridge plan, University Park's commercial developers will lease land from the university under a long-term agreement. At the end of the lease, possession of the land and ownership of the commercial buildings will revert to the university and the state. In addition to university housing, other facilities planned for the University Park campus include a stadium, art gallery, theatrical recital hall, media entertainment center, training conference center, aerospace/advanced technology center, child care facility, recreation center, botanical gardens, and a landscaping green belt.

This innovative development concept will enable CSU-Northridge to proceed with an integrated, multiuse campus development on an accelerated time schedule, rather than waiting out the slow, incremental process that often characterizes state capital appropriations.

UNIVERSITY CENTERS. Another educational model that has emerged in some urban areas is the university center, a means of clustering the educational offerings of several institutions at one site.

The University Center at Tulsa and the Auraria Center in Denver are examples of long-standing university centers. The Tulsa center offers educational services from the University of Oklahoma, the University of Oklahoma Health Services Center, Oklahoma State University, Langston University, and Northeastern State University. The Auraria Center includes the University of Colorado at Denver, Metropolitan State College, and the Community College of Denver. Unfortunately, both of these centers have experienced considerable governance and organizational problems. A more recently formed university center is taking shape in Gwinnett County, Georgia, a rapidly growing county strategically located near I-85, northeast of Atlanta. The Georgia Board of Regents partnered the University of Georgia, Georgia State University and DeKalb College to provide the diverse educational needs of this burgeoning area.

Forty-seven percent of Gwinnett County's population have attended college, and 46 percent of adult residents hold professional or managerial positions. Yet, until the establishment of this university center in 1987, no formalized higher education presence existed in the county.

Like many other states, during the 1960s and early 1970s Georgia established colleges in less populated areas. Unfortunately, these locations were not in the path of population growth, and thus remain beyond the reach of today's emerging urban villages. Moreover, while the state legislature is controlled by Democrats, Gwinnett County's political leaders are Republican. Political support at the state level for an expensive new higher education presence in Gwinnett County has therefore been less than enthusiastic.

The Georgia Board of Regents was forced to respond to Gwinnett County's pressing educational needs with a non-conventional proposal. The traditional method of gradually developing a graduate level institution from a two-year college would not have met the immediate professional development needs of the area's sophisticated and college-educated population. Further, the option of suspending employment or commuting lengthy distances to obtain more education or retraining was simply not practical for the county's many professional and managerial workers.

At the Gwinnett Center, DeKalb College, Georgia's largest multi-campus community college, provides lower-division instruction, fiscal and administrative service support, plus library and computing resources. Georgia State University offers undergraduate courses in the arts, sciences, and business, as well as graduate level business and education courses. The University of Georgia, headquartered thirty five miles away in Athens, has focused on graduate and undergraduate education courses for the county's 5,000 teachers.

In a cooperative venture of this kind, particularly among historically competitive institutions, communication and resolution of potential conflicts are essential to successful operations. Development of coordinated policies and procedures is especially challenging, particularly given the traditional governance and bureaucratic structure of participating institutions. In spite of concerted efforts to remain student- rather than institution-centered, the constant threats of competitive duplication, lack of student accessibility, and other bureaucratic inefficiencies appear to be realities the Gwinnett Center has yet to resolve.

Thus, the university center holds potential as an effective mechanism for combining the resources of existing institutions in a multi-institutional center, capable of providing broader program offerings than any single institution, accessible within a short commuting distance, and cost-effective in the use of public tax dollars. Unfortunately, however, the organizational and funding problems of some existing centers erode their credibility as effective organizational models. A future variation on the university center model may likely utilize an existing institution or branch in an urban area as a learning center that brokers specialized courses and programs from out-of-region institutions.

TARGETED HIGH-TECH CENTERS. As an alternative to branch campuses and university centers, a county with potential rapid growth may establish a targeted educational center, designed to address the specific focused needs of the high tech industry it hopes to cultivate.

The Educational Center at Shady Grove, just outside Washington, D.C. in suburban Montgomery County, Maryland, is a case in point. At least three major ingredients contributed to the development of this significant higher education presence.

First, Montgomery County set aside a 250-acre parcel of land to develop a biotechnology and health science complex—a $38 million total investment including land, infrastructure and buildings. With a hospital already in place on the site and considerable interest expressed by leading biotechnology firms, county leaders offered the package as an incentive to encourage both Johns Hopkins University and the University of Maryland to provide a targeted set of educational offerings complementing the limited lower division programs already offered by Montgomery County College.

Secondly, Montgomery County officials provided leadership and financial support to foster a "can do" attitude that resulted in quicker responsiveness, greater commitment, and larger financial contributions than would have been possible with typical state funding procedures.

Finally, area business leaders played a catalytic role in the project by pressing adamantly for a significant university presence in Montgomery County. Representatives of large and small businesses alike argued that the lack of higher education opportunities compromised the county's quality of life, despite the area's strong commercial and residential fabric.

As a result, Johns Hopkins University began offering graduate instruction at Montgomery County College while awaiting completion of a $9.2 million facility, the centerpiece of its Shady Grove Educational Center. Currently, the Johns Hopkins programs—designed to be self-supporting from the start—focus on graduate engineering, public health, and continuing education. Eventually, Johns Hopkins plans to establish a significant research center at Shady Grove, based on a discipline of strong interest to the area's high-tech businesses.

Meanwhile, the University of Maryland initiated a continuing education program at the county's nearby Police and Fire Training Facility, providing a variety of course offerings from its University College extension program and from its College Park curriculum. The university is also developing extensive biotechnology research and service programs at Shady Grove. Montgomery County has provided the university with a 50-acre tract, infrastructure development and funding for an $8 million building to house the University of Maryland's Center for Advanced Research in Biotechnology. In time, the Shady Grove Educational Center will undoubtedly become the hub for educational, cultural and economic opportunities in Montgomery County.

THE DISTRIBUTED INTERACTIVE UNIVERSITY. Perhaps the most recent and innovative approach to serving expanding metropolitan areas is the concept of the distributed, interactive university, as typified by George Mason University in Fairfax County, Virginia. With the nation's capital at its doorstep, George Mason has gained a reputation for innovation and experimentation in its efforts to meet the demands of a growing network of satellite cities rooted in the vigorous knowledge-based economy of Northern Virginia.

From its beginning in 1960 as a branch campus of the University of Virginia, George Mason has expanded into the nation's fastest growing university. Intent on becoming a prototypical decentralized university, highly interactive with regional government and the high-tech service industry, the institution has focused its development on liberal arts and science programs at the undergraduate level, with graduate and research concentrations in public policy, clean engineering technologies, and the fine and performing arts.

Faced with tremendous demand over the past decade for expanded enrollment and services, George Mason University has undertaken a novel approach to urban service. After evaluating the responses to metropolitan growth by universities around the nation, George Mason is attempting to establish a "distributed" network of geographically distinct "nodes," linked to one another and to the mother campus in Fairfax. Although located at various sites throughout Northern Virginia, each of these "nodes" will feature a world-class research and teaching faculty designated to serve the entire region while remaining an integral part of the university.

Having gained the support of Northern Virginia's leading corporations, politicians, and citizens, George Mason relies on the strategy of recruiting prominent faculty from leading research universities by means of endowed chairs. Organized into centers and institutes, these faculty in turn develop prestigious instructional and research programs, often with an innovative, cross-disciplinary emphasis.

The first widely acclaimed example of these centers was the Center for the Study of Public Choice. Led by 1986 Nobel Laureate James Buchanan, this economic think tank was designed to restructure economic thinking about the functioning of government, bureaucracy, and politics. Another example is the recent creation of the Institute for Performing Arts, which grew out of the former academic departments of music and theatre. The institute is housed in a new 2,000-seat performing arts center on the main Fairfax campus.

George Mason's proposed Prince William Institute is intended as a "vertical slice" of a modern interactive university, featuring all the major components of a comprehensive graduate/research institution: undergraduate and graduate instruction, research, and public service. From the beginning, the institute's programs will serve all of northern Virginia rather than only the current educational needs of Prince William County, where it will be located.

George Mason also plans to build a major complex on its five-acre site in Arlington County, currently home for its law school. The new complex will also house the Institute of International Transactions. Moreover, the University has leased space in Virginia's recently completed Center for Innovative Technology near Dulles Airport. By developing centers and institutes at these and other sites within twenty miles of the Fairfax mother campus, George Mason University is developing the expertise and technical know-how to expand its offerings and services to other regional locations throughout Virginia.

These multiple locations throughout the Northern Virginia region are designed to interconnect via a state-of-the-art telecommunications network. This linkage will position George Mason to expand its offerings to corporate training centers, government agencies, schools, and libraries throughout the region. Such a distributed model may well overcome the difficulties inherent in building a sufficient critical mass of resources, while avoiding the "second class" stigma often attached to university branch campuses. George Mason intends to bypass these problems by utilizing alternate faculty appointment contracts, telecommunications and other means of instructional delivery, supported by creative funding arrangements with local governments and industry.

In short, the George Mason distributed, interactive model may well combine the best features of the targeted high-tech center and the university center, while avoiding the organizational problems of the latter, thus becoming the prototypical model for universities serving hypergrowth metropolitan areas.

SHAPING THE UNIVERSITY
OF THE TWENTY-FIRST CENTURY

The decade of the 1990s will provide both challenges and opportunities destined to shape the sorts of universities that exist as we embark upon the twenty-first century.

On one hand, the educational problems of inner cities will increase as energetic metropolitan growth and development shifts to the emerging suburban downtowns. These urban villages will wield even more significant social, cultural, political and educational influence by this decade's end. On the state level, many states have entered the 1990s with their resources stretched thin, leaving little available funding for new ventures in higher education, no matter how worthy. Nationally, economic growth will be less robust than in recent years, at least during the early 1990s, and much of the attention devoted to education will focus on the highly troubled sectors of elementary and secondary education, rather than postsecondary education.

On the other hand, several factors may provide education with splendid opportunities over the next decade. First, interaction between higher education, industry, and government will continue to grow. American universities will encounter unparalleled opportunities for partnerships, including alliances with universities and multinational corporations from all over the world. Second, coming advances and applications in digital technology, when compounded with recent gains in the use of computing and telecommunications on most campuses, could profoundly affect higher education's practice of research, instruction, and public service.

Though educators have touted the impact of technology on education for years, the results have yet to prove very significant. Over the next decade, however, applications of digital technology could revolutionize the classroom, fundamentally altering patterns and types of interactions between students, faculty, researchers, community problem solvers, and other constituents of colleges and universities. Interactive multimedia, including video discs, compact disc–read only memory (CD-ROM), high-definition television, and advanced computer simulation techniques will be infused into academic instruction. Equally important, advanced technology will allow students, faculty, and researchers in colleges and universities to interact in collaborative learning and problem solving with colleagues at other institutions and in other organizations. Stand-alone learning centers will become outmoded and irrelevant as colleges and universities link together to form a network of learners and researchers. The adaptability and complexity of these emerging organizations must be far greater than that of today's academic organizations.

As these changes alter the shape of American higher education, many colleges and universities located in metropolitan areas will step to the forefront of the search for organizational models of the prototypical twenty-first century university. Often, traditional colleges and universities are insufficiently adaptable to consider adopting new modes of operation, let alone developing new models that deviate significantly from conventional approaches. Metropolitan universities, however, especially those in hypergrowth areas, have already integrated pervasive change into standard patterns of operation and accepted the notion of institutional interaction with the community. These metropolitan institutions are thus well equipped to participate in the development of new approaches to educational delivery. In particular, the development of multi-node universities in metropolitan areas heralds the day when all major universities become to some extent "distributed organizations."

By the twenty-first century, all universities interested in joining international networks for research and instruction will have made great strides toward that participation. Boundaries around colleges and universities will become highly permeable, fostering rich patterns of interaction among faculty and researchers, students, community problem solvers, and other interested parties. The stand-alone campus will have lost its preeminence. The most intensive interaction will occur in metropolitan areas—in this country and all around the world—as metropolitan universities become focal points for international networking. Thus, the emergence of new educational models in hypergrowth metropolitan areas is but a part of the process by which American educational organizations are adapting to the significant changes that accompany the development of a global society.

16

The Distributed University

The year is 2003. On a crisp morning, you leave your home in Manassas for the nearby Prince William Institute, one of several institutes in the George Mason University network. You attend a class in your urban systems engineering program, an interdisciplinary degree that has brought together experts in several areas, including urban planning, real estate development, public policy, and civil engineering.

Your next class is held at the Fairfax (Virginia) campus, but that's no problem for you; there's a video room down the hall that allows you to participate in the lecture without leaving Prince William. After class, you use one of the institute's computers to have a library book sent to you from the Arlington Institute. Heading home you realize that you forgot to drop off a paper, so you send it through your personal computer when you get home.

Sound hard to believe? Such a scenario may become a reality in George Mason's future. The university is now embarking on a plan to create a network of George Mason institutes, known as the "distributed university," throughout Northern Virginia. In this model, each institute, like nodes on a computer network, is linked by telecommunications systems that can access the facilities of all the institutes on the network. This massive undertaking is an attempt to provide education of equal quality to all areas of the region, and to develop interdisciplinary research and programs aimed at solving the region's—and the nation's—most timely problems.

From "The University of the Future" by Maureen Mayer

The idea of a distributed university is not new. Thomas Jefferson is said to have suggested a set of colleges within a day's ride of each

Virginian, all tied to the state's capstone institution, the University of Virginia. It is highly unlikely that Jefferson ever used the word "network", but his concept describes just such an educational system. Later, the land grant college, through its network of county agents, emerged as a special type of American institution designed to distribute knowledge from the university to the agriculture industry. In addition, some of the many universities and colleges that established branch campuses during the last seventy-five years have from time to time taken on the appearance of a network, especially multicampus community colleges, such as the system in Dallas County, Texas.

But none of these illustrations exemplifies an educational network that allows individuals to access the complete range of courses and other services (including library, computing, campus mail, course advising, and registration) characteristic of the modern American university. Today, however, technology and the knowledge age requirement that each person participate in the educational process for life, demand such educational services, giving new force to the idea of a distributed university. Because of changing demographic patterns, large numbers of people now live in urban villages. Increasing numbers of others live in areas of decreasing density. All require lifelong education. Obviously, higher education must look for new forms and approaches to address these twenty-first-century needs.

HISTORICAL HIGHER EDUCATION

Originally, American colleges were founded in remote areas, free from distractions, where it was hoped learners and scholars could evolve into an ideal residential and intellectual community. One early Harvard University president believed so strongly in the educational value of such communities that he once remarked that he would rather build dormitories than classrooms. Of course, the residential colleges situated (or distributed) around the great English universities Oxford and Cambridge provided an early example of effective education resulting from students and teachers living in community. Even that American invention, the land grant college, was usually placed in remote locations within each state in the interest of creating a similar cloistered learning environment.

After industrialization (1870–1920), however, city colleges and universities emerged. These institutions reflected the urban development of the time, i.e., a core city surrounded by suburbia and exurbia. City colleges began in central city areas, and later, as populations spread, established branch campuses and extension centers. But none of these offshoots were considered part of a network, or even a real part of the main institution. Rather, these campuses and extension centers bore the stigma of second-class institutions.

CHANGING EDUCATIONAL DEMAND

But the world is changing. Urban development has abandoned the central city/suburbia/exurbia concept in favor of urban villages, multiple concentrations of office, shopping, residential, and recreational facilities. Tied together by telecommunications and transportation, these large enclaves are heavy consumers of information and education. (See chapter 1.)

Because of work hours, traffic congestion, and other logistic factors characteristic of urban villages, however, main university campuses are becoming less convenient, therefore less accessible, to the learner. Yet, second-class operations such as branch campuses or extension centers are increasingly unacceptable to the sophisticated new American knowledge worker. Thus, the idea of a distributed university is gaining popularity in many fast-growing areas around the country, particularly in Washington, D.C., Atlanta, Southern California, South Florida, and other postindustrial locations where the urban village concept is developing. (See chapter 15.)

The distributed university theory can find applications in other settings as well. Far from the teeming urban villages, areas with sparse and widely-distributed populations also face the fundamental question of how to effectively distribute high quality educational services. In Alaska, for example, low college attendance rates among native Alaskans, who represent the bulk of that state's dispersed population, imply a disinclination toward higher education, making it doubly imperative to deliver high quality, accessible education to potential students where they live. Realistically, only highly motivated learners can be expected to travel great distances for educational services.

The distributed university concept can also meet the growing need for lifelong education. Engineers, for example, now require continuing advanced education throughout their productive careers. Yet, not all industrial locations can offer a full range of graduate engineering or continuing education opportunities. To fill this gap, a new institution was born in 1985. The National Technological University, a consortium of several renowned engineering colleges, is headquartered at Colorado State University. Its goal is to offer first-rate master's level courses and engineering degrees via satellite television. In addition, many other engineering schools are now offering advanced work by means of interactive television—one-way video and two-way audio. This experiment is apparently working well.

Other forces affecting the organization and delivery of high quality educational programs and services that argue for the distributed university concept include the impending faculty shortage and, most importantly, the force of technological development. Most knowledgeable educators agree that in time technology will transform the way people teach and learn. The continuing advancement of computers, telecommunications, and other products of the information age is destined to impact higher education. The challenge for colleges and universities is to learn to maximize technology before new institutions and forms emerge to meet the educational needs of the twenty-first-century and learning flees the academy.

THE THEORY OF DISTRIBUTION

Theoretical discussion of the distributed university has been around for decades. For years academicians have discussed and debated the merits of the centralized versus the decentralized library. Which is best, they question, one major library facility or a core library supporting several strategically-located branch libraries around campus? The fundamental question in this ongoing debate is how to create a critical mass of learning resources while at the same time distributing those resources to the users.

This same debate has surfaced from time to time in regard to computers and computing. In this case, however, the development of the microchip has made it possible to centrally amass major computing capability while distributing significant capabilities to individual users via ever-more-powerful microcomputers. The major challenge in computing now is networking, i.e., how to unite both centralized and decentralized computing into one powerful communications and computing network.

Another recent advancement in distribution is the use of the facsimile (fax) machine, a phenomenon that has grown dramatically in the past few years. Universities with only one fax machine five years ago now employ hundreds of faxes in cross-campus mail networks. Engineering firms, too, are using the fax machine and other telecommunications devices to coordinate work from several locations hundreds of miles apart as easily as from offices just down the hall. In fact, one big-city engineering firm with huge backlogs of work found it simpler and more cost-effective to buy a smaller engineering firm in another city and fax designs back and forth than to hire a sufficient number of engineers at the home office. Such recent quantum leaps in computing and networking are illustrative of the technological advances that make the idea of a distributed university thinkable.

A REAL LIFE MODEL: BELL LABS

As technology advances and becomes more commonplace, the potential for its use in education becomes more practical, even mandatory; the idea of distributing a university over a geographical area becomes more feasible. In fact, there is already an example of a distributed knowledge age institution that provides a good model for colleges and universities—AT&T's Bell Laboratories.

Those who know of Bell Labs recognize this prestigious enterprise as America's premier research institution, the workplace of Nobel laureates and the birthplace of many now ubiquitous inventions, including the transistor, the laser, the solar cell, the communication satellite, and sound motion pictures.

But what is Bell Labs? A large building filled with busy scientists running around in white coats? Or, perhaps, a campus of laboratory buildings? In reality, Bell Labs is a distributed network of research facilities with several major laboratories located in New Jersey and other states. There is no main building versus branch labs. Scientists who have won Nobel prizes for work done at Bell Labs have operated from several different facilities. Bell Labs is, in fact, a working network of research facilities or nodes tied together with modern communications. This network provides each person at each location with access to the same resources and the same information. In reality, Bell Labs is a distributed institution that can serve as an excellent model for institutions of higher education looking to the twenty-first-century.

CANDIDATES FOR THE DISTRIBUTED UNIVERSITY

Which American institution will become the nation's first distributed university? There are currently several candidates, including the University of Alaska and George Mason University in Fairfax, Virginia.

In Alaska, the state university has been restructured from a system of three university branch campuses and eleven community colleges plus other facilities into three university centers. Each center offers multiple sites and a broad range of programs, and each bears responsibility for remote sites. In reality, each of these three university centers is a distributed network of educational sites. Given the proper context and the appropriate use of technology, these centers could take the form of a twenty-first-century distributed university.

Whether or not this evolution occurs rests on questions of strategy and will. Alaska is a frontier where the limits and possibilities of distribution theory can be tested; with its great distances and its sparse, dispersed population, it is a state whose very future depends on solving the educational problems the distributed university theory is designed to address. Alaska is an obvious candidate for a great educational experiment.

Across the continent in Virginia, George Mason University stands at the other extreme. Surrounded by 1.4 million people living within a thirty-mile radius of its main campus, George Mason is challenged to overcome problems of transportation and community organization as they affect the delivery of educational programs and services. The Northern Virginia region that George Mason serves now includes eight major urban villages, with more sure to develop during the twenty-first-century. Severe transportation problems make it difficult for this area's education-hungry populace to commute to the university's main campus in Fairfax.

The George Mason plan for a distributed university includes creating a parallel academic organization consisting of institutes—located both on and off the Fairfax campus—that combine departments, schools, colleges, and centers. Thus far, an institute for the arts has been organized on the Fairfax campus to replace the performing arts departments. This institute has assumed the additional responsibilities of managing the university's new $30 million Center for the Arts and of implementing an innovative university-wide arts education program. Also located on the Fairfax campus are the Robinson Professors Program, consisting of twenty endowed professorships for distinguished scholars committed to teaching undergraduates and building a modern university, and the Krasnow Institute for Advanced Study, an endowed interdisciplinary research institute.

George Mason's Arlington, Virginia campus houses the Institute for International Transactions, headed by economist John Moore, former deputy director of the National Science Foundation. Also sharing the Arlington site is the university's law school and its noted Center for Law and Economics. Twenty miles to the west of Fairfax, George Mason is currently working with Prince William County to establish the Prince William Institute, designed to offer an array of degree and credential programs, including a school for urban systems engineering, an executive MBA, plus graduate and undergraduate courses and programs as needed. Other institutes, to be located both on the Fairfax campus and elsewhere, are under consideration. All will to be tied together in a communications and service network, with faculty stationed at one site, but carrying responsibilities for other sites and programs as well.

The nature of these institutes raises many concerns: Where does a faculty member involved at several centers receive tenure? How does a distributed university achieve the degree of nodal democracy evident at Bell Labs? Can these different nodes be tied together electronically? Can the educational establishment make the adjustments necessary to maximize emerging technologies in the interest of better education for all Americans?

Whatever the ultimate answer to these questions, clearly a major educational experiment is underway at Virginia's George Mason University. If nothing else, this experiment will test the validity and accepted context of traditional American higher education.

In summary, demographics, technology, and the empowerment offered by education in the new science-driven economy will come together into one powerful force destined to restructure higher education in America. The main question to be answered as this scenario unfolds is: Will colleges and universities lead America into the future with innovation, experiments, and pilot programs, or will they be painfully forced into the new century?

17

Summary and Conclusions

It was Frederick Jackson Turner who proposed the historical theory that America has always defined and redefined itself by pushing out its frontiers. Building on that idea, Vannevar Bush, former MIT vice president and founder of both the Raytheon Corporation and the National Science Foundation, believed the frontiers of science would define America after World War II. Writing in the July 1945 *Atlantic Monthly*, Bush argued that the real post-war scientific challenge would be the management of information.[1] As it happened, Bush was accurate in predicting a science-driven world economy that would result in an information or knowledge age. He was also correct in assuming this development would define America in the twenty-first century.

The new economic era predicted by Bush nearly half a century ago is today turning the world upside down. As the 1990s opened, socialism—an invention of industrial age theorists who believed human beings could be maneuvered like chunks of ore or drums of chemicals—was collapsing around the world. Even in the Soviet Union, new economic forces and the unfettered movement of ideas across national borders are upending long-held certainties. New economic powers are surfacing, and old ones—Japan and Germany—are reemerging. The United States no longer sits alone atop the pyramid of economically powerful nations. Ironically, our nation, just a few short decades ago the envy of the world, is now struggling both economically and educationally. In fact, many observers question whether or not we are in decline.

The 1990s are destined to be a period of great change, a transition from the industrial age to the new information economy, and a time when education will be crucial in assuring the economic competitiveness of America and other developed nations. Yet American schoolchildren of every age group rank no better than average in performance compared to their peers in nations with major economic power.

The demands of the new era are already wreaking havoc on the social fabric of the nation. Families are breaking up, and children living in single-parent households today, on average, fare less well economically than a generation ago. Demographically, America is changing rapidly. The number of young workers, those whose taxes must pay for most ongoing social programs, is declining, yet older workers and retirees resist any reduction in their social benefits, as well as any new taxes for infrastructure improvements. Added to these changes is the impact of fast-growing minority groups, now quickly becoming the majority.

America's 3,200 colleges and universities face a dilemma in the decade of the 1990s. Still the nation's most desired international product, American higher education is clearly challenged to do even more—perhaps with less—in the decades ahead. The agenda begins with an accumulation of educational issues, the legacy of inaction or excesses during the 1980s, that now demand immediate action. Higher education must also adjust to a turnaround in the nation's management of colleges and universities, a shift in focus from the federal level to the state capitals. At the same time, colleges and universities must retool to meet the emerging needs of a new science-driven economy that is reshaping America, creating thriving new postindustrial economic centers, while other regions suffer decline or dormancy.

This book has addressed six major issues now facing American higher education, examined the relationship of the states and higher education, and considered new forms of higher education now developing in response to changing demographics, technology, and economic conditions. (Other concerns not covered here must also be addressed during the coming decade. These include possible institutional roles in public school reform and the subject of accountability, including assessment.) Careful study of the topics discussed in this volume has yielded a number of conclusions and recommendations.

To begin, minority participation in higher education must be given the highest priority by local and state governments, corporations and foundations, and each of the 3200 colleges and universities in this nation. Many innovative approaches to minority education at every level promise success, but to ensure quality education for America's growing minority population, these concepts must be united in an immediate nationwide educational strategy akin to the

Marshall Plan. No longer only a matter of equity as perceived in the 1960s, the issue of minority education has become a matter of national economic survival. The quality of the American work force in the twenty-first century will depend on the quality of education available to all Americans in the 1990s and beyond.

Changes in institutional, state, and national policies are necessary to replace quality faculty and mitigate the serious faculty shortage predicted as the glut of professors hired during the 1960s and 1970s approaches retirement age. Existing early retirement programs exacerbate this predicament, robbing both industry and the academy of prime talent, especially in numerous fields where distinctive skills and experience have become valuable commodities. While retirement benefits cannot be abrogated, we must find ways to keep the most productive members of our veteran work force engaged. Further, now is the time to fill the faculty pipeline by encouraging young academics, a task that requires national attention as well as institutional will. The academic life must be accorded new value and respect in order to attract the best and brightest of today's students. Appropriate levels of prestige and remuneration may also help recruit former academics and retirees from business and government, bridging the gap between faculty retirements and replacements from the pipeline.

With the days of easy money now behind them, colleges and universities must develop new fiscal approaches in order to finance quality higher education. Governments pressed by mounting demands for increased social services have pushed higher education down the ladder of funding priorities. At the same time, much political concern now revolves around escalating tuition and fees (previously rendered acceptable by once-abundant federally guaranteed student loans), which financed many institutional improvements in the 1980s. Thus, the academy is on the horns of a dilemma, requiring more resources even as traditional funding sources disappear.

Many institutions are successfully pursuing the strategy of selective excellence in order to maximize their fiscal resources. These schools have decided to focus scarce resources on chosen areas of excellence, rather than spreading themselves too thin in a futile attempt to be everything to everyone. Athletic departments operating by the principle of selective excellence, for example, may allot varying funds to three tiers of programs, concentrating sufficient resources for national competition (and national reputations) only on their strongest sports teams. A number of universities are pursuing similar tactics to build or rebuild academic reputations. The strategy of selective excellence may emerge as one of the most significant movements in American higher education in the 1990s.

Realizing the goal of affordable higher education requires both institutions and society to grapple with a number of critical questions. Will cost-benefit economics eventually cause students to turn away from college? Is it fair that middle-income students must obtain and repay huge loans to meet inflated tuition costs, while low-income students are subsidized with grants taken from those payments? Will a declining population of young workers be willing to provide tax support for entitlement programs after mortgaging their futures to obtain their own economic skills? Will some future economic recession convert tens of billions of dollars in government-backed student loans into a fiscal crisis rivalling the savings and loan debacle? When does providing a college education to a generation of young people become a general societal responsibility?

While questions proliferate, answers are few. American families must return to the early habit of saving for college expenses, while legislators should explore the possibility of national service in exchange for educational benefits.

Seduced, like other elements of society, by the 1980s maxim "greed is good," American colleges and universities must now act in consort to affirm new standards of institutional ethics. Over the past decade, the hunger for private money, public/private partnerships, and national recognition led many college and university officials into questionable endeavors and practices. Corruption in intercollegiate athletics, manipulation of research standings, and fraudulent indicators of student body performance have damaged more than just those institutions involved; the entire academy stands in real danger of suffering discredit. To reverse this dangerous trend, accrediting agencies should activate new ethical standards. National associations of higher education, as well as individual institutions, should also set clear, firm criteria of policy and conduct.

American higher education also bears a major responsibility for national economic development. A trained and educated work force is an imperative if the United States is to maintain national economic competitiveness in the global marketplace of the twenty-first century. The nation's leadership in basic and applied research will remain another critical factor in economic development. Research institutions must therefore continue or even redouble their efforts, while speeding and improving methods of technology transfer. Finally, all colleges and universities need up-to-date laboratories in order to keep abreast of tremendous changes and advancements in technology.

The community college perspective on these issues, as presented by Dr. George B. Vaughan, often mirrors the concerns of four-year institutions. A true invention of American higher education, community colleges originated after World War II in response to demands for technical training and increased access to college level education. Now over 1,200 strong, community colleges are strategically located throughout the nation, in every major population center and hundreds of rural areas. Well-suited to help solve many of higher education's pressing concerns for the 1990s, community colleges offer particular strengths in educating minorities and maintaining affordability. On the other hand, community colleges often lack funding sources generally available to four-year institutions, and their expansion during the 1960s and 1970s ensures increased faculty replacement problems on the horizon.

As higher education adjusts its focus from Washington, D.C. to the state capitals, where the most significant education-related policy now originates, administrators must strive to bridge a growing communications gap between governors and college and university presidents. Institution presidents must work harder, communicate better, and, above all, respond more sensitively to major social problems facing the states and their government leaders.

Profiles of four politicians who earned reputations as education governors offer insight into successful state education reform movements. Former governors Thomas Kean, Bill Clinton, Lamar Alexander and Robert Graham all came to office convinced of the critical link between education and economic development and determined to improve public education. All persevered despite significant opposition, achieving marked progress in educational quality in their states.

A profile of excellence in state higher education emerges from survey research revealing secrets of the best state university systems. Analysis of the top ten systems (as determined by the 1988–89 CPSE survey responses of governors, college presidents, and other higher education professionals) indicates a number of common denominators, including significant minority and doctoral enrollments, low in-state and out-of-state migration, strong faculty support, solid financial backing, and the presence of a nationally recognized flagship university. Overall, success seems to follow an institutional mindset that values high ideals and institutional distinctiveness.

In addition to traditional contributions in education and research, America's institutions of higher education are uniquely qualified to offer society valuable insight into managing knowledge age organizations. Generally speaking, American colleges and universities have been much better administered than is commonly perceived. As the first of the knowledge industries, higher education fell victim to charges of poor management by industrial age standards.

But in a postindustrial world, where research corporations, government laboratories, large law firms, and health maintenance organizations are gaining recognition as second-generation knowledge industries, higher education can win respect as a management model for the new economic environment.

A less positive development affecting higher education is the trend toward increasing politicization. State higher education executive officers, for example, now often emerge from political, rather than academic, backgrounds. In most cases, however, these appointments have been good ones.

The bulk of political static can be traced to byzantine state coordinating boards. Still enforcing five-year plans even after the Soviets have discarded the concept, these bodies maintain rigid political postures regarding educational planning. In an era of perpetual change, however, institutions must be free to respond quickly and boldly to the evolving needs of their constituents. Coordinating boards must therefore develop the flexibility to allow, even encourage, this freedom.

Governing boards of multicampus university systems can especially benefit from an academic strategy that promotes institutional distinctiveness. Within a system-wide context established by the board, individual institutions can develop unique strategies to maximize their peculiar strengths, and simultaneously lend distinction to the system as a whole.

America's entrance into a new age dominated by science, technology, and information sparked early and significant changes in many of the nation's metropolitan areas. In response to the evolving needs of these burgeoning economic centers, higher education is developing new ways of serving hypergrowth regions. Detailed by Edward L. Delaney and Donald M. Norris, these approaches include customized programs of study; professional, rather than academic, instructors; innovative administrative structures; technology use; community involvement; public/private partnerships; enhanced institutional cooperation; quality of life components; and accelerated institutional development.

One of the most promising new concepts in higher education is that of the distributed university. The fundamentals of this theory recall a long-discussed quandary of higher education—how to simultaneously amass library resources and distribute them to users. Of course, with the advent of the microchip, it is now possible to develop and distribute massive computing power from a central data bank through a network of personal computers. But can education power be similarly amassed and distributed to distant users via advanced technology? Why not? Several institutions now stand on the threshold of demonstrating the validity and value of the distributed university concept in a rapidly evolving postindustrial society. Any one of these institutions could emerge as the prototypical twenty-first century university.

In summary, the 1990s will be a decade of challenge for higher education. Difficult issues must be confronted and managed. Stronger bonds must be forged with government and society. Flexible planning strategies must be developed.By thinking about these challenges, college and university leaders can mentally prepare to respond quickly and boldly in the face of perpetual change, i.e., to adapt. And adaptability will be a key determinant of survival for the American higher education establishment in the twenty-first century.

Appendix: 1988–89 Survey of Higher Education

Conducted by
Center for Policy Studies in Education
George Mason University, Fairfax, Virginia

This study was conducted in the fall of 1988 and winter of 1989. Two hundred fifty college and university presidents, governors, and others familiar with American higher education were asked to complete the ten-page, eleven-item questionnaire. The college and university presidents survey included the 100 universities sampled in the 1987–88 survey plus fifty community college presidents. Eighty-eight, or 58 percent of the presidents; twenty-nine, or 58 percent of the governors; and thirty-one, or 62 percent of the remainder (professors of higher education, association heads, and others) responded by completing the questionnaire. The overall response rate was 148 out of 250, or 59 percent. No effort was made to distinguish between the respondents except by the three original categories.

Question 1. What do you believe to be the three (or more, if you choose) overriding issues/problems facing American higher education as we approach a new century?

Governors' Top Issues

PRIMARY

Affordable higher education, costs to students
Minority participation
Helping the United States keep the competitive edge
Assessment/accountability

Financing quality education
Restructuring teacher education
Keeping up with changes in technology
Replacing quality faculty

Presidents' Top Issues

PRIMARY

Financing quality education
Minority participation
Replacing quality faculty
Affordable higher education

SECONDARY

Keeping up with technological change
America's competitive edge
Governance/Leadership
Assessment/Accountability
Broadly educating the population with quality programs

Others' Top Issues

Affordable higher education
Minority participation
Financing quality
Replacing quality faculty

Overall Top Issues:

PRIMARY

Minority participation
Replacing quality faculty
Financing quality education
Affordable higher education

SECONDARY

Assessment/Accountability
Helping the United States keep competitive edge

Governance and leadership
Improving public schools

Question 2. What are the three (or more) most powerful factors influencing higher education's development in your local area?

Governors' Top Factors

PRIMARY

Relationship to job market and community demands
Limited financial resources
Poor support of the need for quality education

SECONDARY

Low expectations of and for students

Presidents' Top Factors

PRIMARY

Limited fiscal resources
Demographic changes in area
Economy of the area
Relationship to job market and community demands
Poor support of the need for quality education

SECONDARY

"Politicizing" of higher education issues
Reorganization of the governing of higher education and the role
of the state

Others' Top Factors

PRIMARY

Competition with other institutions and areas for students and
faculty
Minority influx/needs of minority students
Politics of higher education issues

Federal financial aid for students
Needed improvements in primary and secondary education

Question 3. Are there troubling behavior patterns emerging in the administration of colleges and universities?

Governors' Troubling Patterns

Incompetency of two- and four-year school administrators
Excessive administrative expenses
Political influence on decisions

Presidents' Troubling Patterns

PRIMARY

Political influence on administrative decision-making
Increased federal regulation, process complexity
Too much public system control
Administration acts expediently, not for the long run

SECONDARY

Externalization of management (to trustees, etc.)
Lack of clear educational direction
High turnover rate in academic administration
Anti-intellectual, anti-quality attitudes among two- and four-year
administrators
Employee litigiousness and resulting wasted funds
Decreasing funding at the state level
Seven college and university presidents felt there are no troubling behavior patterns in administration.

Others' Troubling Patterns

Lack of quality in two- and four-year school administrators
Increased complexity of simple processes due to federal regulation
Too much public system control
No focus on long-term planning, long-term solutions
Failure of administration to address issues
Need to share goals/purposes with faculty and others

Ascendancy of faculty power with no corresponding responsibility

Growing racial tensions

Question 4. Do you see a pattern of state interdiction into the internal operation of state colleges and universities? If so, elaborate.

Thirteen presidents and five others saw no pattern of state interdiction, while twenty-four presidents and ten others said there is interdiction.

Presidents' most commonly cited interdictions

PRIMARY

State centralization of administrative areas and programs

Regulation and standardization of processes

State and gubernatorially set priorities within colleges and universities

Mandated academic assessment

State control of purchases, expenditure limits by category lead to a disregard for institutional individual

Others most often mentioned mandated academic assessment as state interdiction.

Question 5. Please name three important trends which you see as emerging in American higher education.

Governors' Top Trends

More accountability for educational outcome

Closer relationship with government agencies, business, and industry

Growing role of higher education in economic development

Increasing diversity of student body

Increasing costs

Presidents' Top Trends

PRIMARY

Linking of higher education and economic development

Emphasis on quality undergraduate education, back-to-basics attitude

Use of technology
Facing global competitiveness

SECONDARY

Assessment of student learning
Concern for minorities, influx of immigrants
Internationalization of curriculum
Steady increase of continuing, nontraditional and part-time education numbers

Others' Top Trends

Concern for minorities and increasing number of immigrants
Increased emphasis on assessment of student learning and program effectiveness
State involvement, influence, and control at the local level
Use of technology
Linking of higher education and economic development
Lack of restraint on intercollegiate athletics

Question 6. What are the most promising college curriculum developments now in the early stages?

Governors' Most Promising Developments

Computer literacy for all
Increased focus on math/science areas for liberal arts majors
Internationalization of business and technical areas
Teaching the merit of entrepreneurship
Return of foreign language requirements
Centralized curriculum control
Interstate curriculum mergers
Growing interest in liberal arts fields
Use of electronics and technology to maximize course content and access to courses
Across-curriculum teaching of writing and speech
Interdisciplinary exploration of topics
Partnership between professional schools and liberal arts areas
Asian language instruction
Collaboration with job market to create curriculum for specific needs
Teacher education curriculum reforms

More concern by faculty for assessment of the quality and under-
graduate education
Environmental sciences studies
Software and delivery systems

Presidents' Most Promising Developments

PRIMARY

Across-the-board teaching of writing and speech
More attention to core curriculum and general education
Use of electronics and technology to maximize couse content and
access to courses

SECONDARY

Core curriculum innovations/broadening the general education
requirements
Introducing international education—multi-cultural perspec-
tives
International business and foreign relations

Others' Most Promising Developments

More attention to core curriculum and general education
Across-curriculum teaching of speech and writing
Introducing international education with multi-cultural perspec-
tives
Computer literacy for everyone
Return of foreign language requirements
More attention to student assessment in major programs
Area studies

*Question 8. Which states do you admire for the overall quality of
public colleges and universities?*

TOP THREE:

California
North Carolina
Michigan

NEXT SEVEN, ALPHABETICALLY:

Florida
Illinois
Minnesota
New York
Texas
Virginia
Wisconsin

Question 9. Which governors would you recognize for their efforts to improve the quality of public colleges and universities?

Governor Kean, New Jersey
Governor Clinton, Arkansas
Governor Alexander, Tennessee

Question 10. What are the three most critical challenges facing America in the 1990s?

Governors' Challenges

Federal fiscal stability/balancing the national budget
Dealing seriously with environmental problems
Raising America's economic competitiveness
Reversing the growth of the underclass

Presidents' Challenges

Dealing with the federal budget deficit
Educating average and less advantaged people to fill the needs of the labor market
Eliminating the trade deficit
Raising America's economic competitiveness
Social problems
Reversing the growth of an underclass

Others' Challenges

Federal fiscal responsibility
Social problems
Eliminating the trade deficit
Inciting the desire to be competitive and achieve

Dealing with environmental problems
Restoring the United States as a world leader

Question 11. Who can do more to improve the quality of American higher education: the president of the United States, Congress, governors, college/university presidents, business, etc?

MOST COMMON ANSWERS OVERALL WERE:

All of the above
College presidents
Governors
State legislature

Question 12. Do you think that the recent listing of "best" colleges and universities by U.S. News and World Report is of value?

	GOVERNORS	PRESIDENTS	OTHERS	TOTAL
Yes	9	10	2	21
No	4	31	12	47
Somewhat	3	2	0	5
Haven't seen report	0	2	1	3

Do you think this listing is accurate?

	GOVERNORS	PRESIDENTS	OTHERS	TOTAL
Yes	6	2	2	10
No	7	27	12	46
Mostly/maybe	1	4	0	5

Do you think this listing is based on appropriate measures (SAT scores, expenditures per student)?

	GOVERNORS	PRESIDENTS	OTHERS	TOTAL
Yes	6	4	2	10
No	8	31	10	49
Somewhat	0	1	1	2

A more comprehensive set of measures was suggested, including success of the students, the number of Rhodes scholars, and scores on graduate admissions exams.

Notes

Chapter 1

1. Conversation with Michael Hooker, president of the University of Maryland, Baltimore, Maryland, 26 October 1989.
2. *Executive Trend Watch*, Washington, D.C., December 1989, 7.
3. Christopher B. Leinberger and Charles Lockwood, "How Business is Reshaping America," *Atlantic Monthly* 258, no. 4 (October 1986): 43–52.
4. *Trends: Education, Employment, Population—Challenge 2000* (Atlanta: Southern Regional Education Board, 1989).

Chapter 2

1. American Council on Education and Education Commission of the States, *One-Third of a Nation: A Report of the Commission on Minority Participation in Education and American Life* (American Council on Education, and Education Commission of the States, Washington, D.C.: 1988), 2.
2. Fairfax County Public Schools, *Directions for a System in Transition*, (Fairfax, Va.: Fairfax County School Board, 1989), 7–8.
3. Jean Evangelauf, "Minorities' Share of College Enrollments Edges Up, as Number of Asian and Hispanic Students Soars," *Chronicle of Higher Education* 34, no. 26 (9 March 1988): A33.
4. "Fewer Black Men on U.S. Campuses," *New York Times*, 17 January 1989.
5. *One-Third of a Nation*, 11.
6. Martin Haberman, "More Minority Teachers," *Phi Delta Kappan* 70, no. 10 (June 1989): 773.
7. *One-Third of a Nation*, 12–13.
8. William F. Brazziel, "Road Blocks to Graduate School: Black Americans Are Not Achieving Parity," *Educational Record* 68/69, nos. 4/1 (Fall 1987-Winter 1988): 108–109.

9. "Consortium Nurtures a Crop of Scholars," *Educational Record* 68/69, nos. 4/1 (Fall 1987-Winter 1988): 112.

10. Edward B. Fiske, "Colleges Open New Minority Drives," *New York Times*, 18 November 1987.

Chapter 3

1. Karen Grassmuck, "Columbia University Uses Philosophy of 'Selective Excellence' to Make Painful Cuts in Programs, Administration," *Chronicle of Higher Education* 36, no. 32 (25 April 1990): A1.

Chapter 4

1. Robin Wilson, "Bennett's Tenure: Prominence for the Education Department, but Alienation on Capitol Hill and the Campuses," *Chronicle of Education* 35, no. 4 (21 September 1988): A24–25, A28.

2. Janet S. Hansen, "Pay Now. Go Later," *College Board Review* 147 (Spring 1988): 9.

3. Ibid., 8.

4. "Opinion Leaders See Rising College Costs as Major Concern," *Chronicle of Higher Education* 34, no. 24 (24 February 1988): A1.

5. "Students Cite Price as Deterrent to College," *Higher Education & National Affairs* 37, no. 18 (17 October 1988): 5.

6. Kent Halstead, *Higher Education Tuition*, (Washington, D.C.: Research Associates, 1989).

7. Scott Jaschik, "State-College Officials Call Public's Panic Over Fees Needless," *Chronicle of Higher Education* 34, no. 36 (18 May 1988): A1.

8. Garry A. Boulard, "Higher Education Commissioners Urge State Commissioners to Limit Tuition Raises and to Explain Costs to Public," *Chronicle of Higher Education* 35, no. 4 (21 September 1988): A31.

9. "Higher Ed Groups Seek Increases In Student Aid," *Higher Education & National Affairs* 38, no. 9 (8 May 1989): 1.

10. *Trends in Student Aid: 1980 to 1990* (Princeton, N. J.: College Entrance Examination Board, 1990): 3.

11. "Fact File: Trends in Student Aid, 1980–81 to 1987–88" *Chronicle of Higher Education* 35, no. 4 (21 September 1988): A40.

12. Courtney Leatherman, "State Spending on Financial Aid for Needy Students Expected to Total $1.5 Billion This Academic Year," *Chronicle of Higher Education* 35, no. 24 (22 February 1989): A21.

13. "Fact File: Trends in Student Aid, 1980–81 to 1987–88," *Chronicle of Higher Education* 53, no. 4 (21 September 1988): A40.

14. Hansen, 8.

15. Ibid.

16. Troy Murray, "Investment Issues," in *Invitational Conference on Col-*

lege Prepayment and Savings Plans: Proceedings (New York: College Board, 1988).

Chapter 5

1. Howard R. Bowen and Jack H. Schuster, *American Professors: A National Resource Imperiled.* (New York: Oxford University Press, 1986).
2. Carolyn J. Mooney, "Uncertainty Is Rampant as Colleges Begin to Brace for Faculty Shortage Expected to Begin in 1990s," *Chronicle of Higher Education* 35, no. 20 (25 January 1989): A14.
3. Ibid., A16.
4. Ibid.
5. Paul A. Lacey, "Faculty Development and the Future of College Teaching," *New Directions for Teaching and Learning* 33 (Spring 1988): 62.
6. Edward B. Fiske, "Lessons: Attracting Star Professors Starts Sounding Like the Bidding for Top Athletes," *New York Times*, 27 July 1988.
7. Ibid.
8. Lisa W. Foderaro, "Big Name on Campus," *New York Times Magazine*, 8 August 1988.
9. Michael I. Sovern, "Higher Education: The Real Crisis," *New York Times Magazine*, 22 January 1989.

Chapter 6

1. Charles J. Sykes, *Profscam: Professors and the Demise of Higher Education* (New York: Regnery Gateway, 1988).
2. Deirdre Carmody, "Colleges' S.A.T. Lists Can Be Creative Works," *New York Times*, 25 November 1987.

Chapter 7

1. Joseph Berger, "More Businesses and Schools Join to Attack Illiteracy in Workplace," *New York Times*, 8 September 1988.
2. Lee A. Daniels, "Illiteracy Seen as Threat to U.S. Economic Edge," *New York Times*, 7 September 1988.
3. "Trends in Public School Budgets," unpublished report by the Center for Policy Studies in Education, George Mason University, Fairfax, Virginia, 1990.
4. "Practical Uses for Research Needed to Keep U.S. Competitive, Bok Says," *Higher Education & National Affairs* 38, no. 2 (30 January 1989): 1.
5. *Issues in Higher Education and Economic Development* (Washington, D.C.: American Association of State Colleges and Universities, 1986).

Chapter 8

1. Dale Parnell, *Dateline 2000: The New Higher Education Agenda* (Washington, D.C.: Community College Press, 1990), 90.
2. Sonia L. Nazario, "Bearing the Brunt: Community Colleges Must Train Many of the Nation's Workers, But They May Not Be Up to the Job," *Wall Street Journal*, 9 February 1990.
3. Arthur Cohen and Florence Brawer, *The American Community College* (San Francisco: Jossey-Bass, 1989), 137.
4. Robert Templin. "Keeping the Door Open for Disadvantaged Students," in *Issues for Community College Leaders in a New Era*, edited by George B. Vaughan (San Francisco: Jossey-Bass, 1983), 39–54.
5. Mary Crystal Cage, "Tight Funds Thwarting States' Desire to Raise 2-Year-College Quality," *Chronicle of Higher Education* 36, no. 27 (21 March 1990): A26.
6. Walker, Rob, "Graying of Professors Said to Pose Challenge," *Richmond Times-Dispatch*, 13 March 1990.
7. "Inbox," *Chronicle of Higher Education* 36, no. 27 (21 March 1990): A18.
8. George B. Vaughan, *Pathway to the Presidency: The Community College Dean of Instruction* (Washington, D.C.: Community College Press, 1990): 61.

Chapter 9

1. Amy Schwartz, "A New Ivory Tower," *Washington Post* (11 November 1986): 22.
2. Robert Rosenzweig, "Seeing Ourselves as Others See Us," 33, no. 10 *Chronicle of Higher Education* (6 November 1986): 104.
3. J. Wade Gilley and Kenneth A. Fulmer, *A Question of Leadership: or, To Whom Are the Governors Listening?*, unpublished report by the Center for Policy Studies in Education, George Mason University, Fairfax, Virginia.

Chapter 10

1. Thomas H. Kean, "Time for Action: A New Political Consensus," *Change* 18, no. 5 (September-October 1986): 10.
2. Carolyn J. Mooney, "No Joke: Higher Education in New Jersey Thrives Along with State's Booming Economy," *Chronicle of Higher Education* 34, no. 7 (14 October 1987): A20.
3. Thomas H. Kean, "What States Should Do (and Not Do) to Improve Undergraduate Education," *Chronicle of Higher Education* 31, no. 2 (11 September 1985): 128.
4. Frank Newman, "Rising Expectations: Can States Help Renew Quality?" *Change* 17, no. 6 (November-December 1985): 12–15.

5. Ibid., 13.
6. Ibid.
7. Ibid.
8. Mooney, "No Joke," A21.
9. Carolyn J. Mooney, "New Jersey's Kean Embraces Higher-Education Issues with Rare Passion," *Chronicle of Higher Education* 34, no. 27 (14 October 1987): A21, A28.
10. *The Alexander Report*, cited in "A Vision of Excellence: Educational Reform in Arkansas, 1983–1989" (Little Rock: State of Arkansas, Office of the Governor, 1989): 1.
11. Ibid.
12. Susan Tifft, "How to Tackle School Reform," *Time* 134, no. 7 (14 August 1989): 46.
13. *The Alexander Report*, 1.
14. Tifft, 46.
15. Bill Clinton, "Who Will Manage the Schools?" *Phi Delta Kappan* 68 (November 1986): 208.
16. Scott Jaschik, "A Governor Pours Millions More into Education," *Chronicle of Higher Education* 33, no. 1 (3 September 1986): 25.
17. *The Alexander Report*, 1.
18. John Parish, "Excellence in Education: Tennessee's 'Master' Plan," *Phi Delta Kappan* 64 (June 1983): 724.
19. Lamar Alexander, Inaugural Address, 15 January 1983, in *Tennessee Blue Book 1983–1984* (Nashville: State of Tennessee, 1983), 99.
20. Lamar Alexander, "Master Teachers in Tennessee Schools," *American Educator* VII (Winter 1983): 12–14, 42.
21. Hope Aldrich, "The Day the PTA Stayed Home," *Washington Monthly* 16, no. 5 (June 1984): 48.
22. Sheila Wissner, "Higher Education Enjoys a 'Golden Era,'" *Nashville Tennessean*, 31 December 1989.
23. Ibid.
24. Ibid.
25. University of Tennessee, Office of the President, 1990.
26. Wissner.
27. Lamar Alexander, "Time for Results: An Overview," *Phi Delta Kappan* 68 (November 1986): 202–204.
28. "Alexander on Education: The Views of Former Governor, Bush Adviser, and Soon-to-Be University Chief," *Chronicle of Higher Education* 34, no. 39 (8 June 1988): A16.
29. Robert Graham, "The State Role," *Journal of Education Finance* 8 (1982): 138.
30. Ibid.
31. *Education Report Card: A Review of Florida's Accomplishments* (Tallahassee: State of Florida, 1985), 2.

32. "Florida Ranked No. 1 in Improving Public Education," *Tampa Tribune*, 13 May 1984.

33. *Bob Graham, the 38th Governor of Florida* (Tallahassee: State of Florida, Office of the Governor, 1986).

34. Ed Birk, "TaxWatch Says Florida Ranks 13th in Per-Pupil Spending," *Tampa Tribune*, 13 March 1986.

35. *Quest for Excellence: The Master Plan of the State University System of Florida* (Tallahassee: State University System of Florida, 1985), 2.

36. Ibid.

37. *Education Report Card*, 4–5.

38. "Teacher's Union Endorses Graham for U.S. Senate," *Tallahassee Democrat*, 23 June 1986.

Chapter 11

1. Cecilia A. Ottinger, ed., *1986–1987 Fact Book on Higher Education* (New York: ACE/Macmillan, 1987).

Chapter 12

1. "The Worst Thing Is to Modernize," *U.S. News and World Report* 102, no. 4 (2 February 1987): 23.

2. Conversation with D. Quinn Mills, professor at the Harvard Graduate School of Business, Cambridge, Mass., 2 June 1989.

Chapter 14

1. Richard L. Alfred and Julie Weissman, *Higher Education and the Public Trust: Improving Stature in Colleges and Universities*, ASHE-ERIC Higher Education Report No. 6 (Washington, D.C.: Association for the Study of Higher Education, 1987).

Chapter 17

1. Vannevar Bush, "As We May Think," *Atlantic Monthly* (July 1945).

References

Chapter 1

Executive Trend Watch. Washington, D.C., December 1989, 7.

Hooker, Michael. Conversation with the author, Baltimore, Maryland, 26 October 1989.

Leinberger, Christopher B., and Lockwood, Charles. "How Business Is Reshaping America." *Atlantic Monthly* 258, no. 4 (October 1986): 43–52.

Trends: Education, Employment, Population—Challenge 2000. Atlanta: Southern Regional Education Board, 1989.

Chapter 2

American Council on Education and Education Commission of the States. *One-Third of a Nation: A Report of the Commission on Minority Participation in Education and American Life*. Washington, D.C.: American Council on Education and Education Commission of the States, 1988.

Brazziel, William F. "Road Blocks to Graduate School: Black Americans Are Not Achieving Parity." *Educational Record* 68/69, nos. 41 (Fall 1987-Winter 1988): 108–111, 113–115.

"Consortium Nurtures a Crop of Scholars." *Educational Record* 68/69, nos. 41 (Fall 1987-Winter 1988): 112.

Evangelauf, Jean. "Minorities' Share of College Enrollments Edges Up, as Number of Asian and Hispanic Students Soars." *Chronicle of Higher Education* 34, no. 26 (9 March 1988): A33ff.

Fairfax County Public Schools. *Directions for a System in Transition*. Fairfax, Va.: Fairfax County School Board, 1989.

"Fewer Black Men on U.S. Campuses." *New York Times*, 17 January 1989.

Fiske, Edward B. "Colleges Open New Minority Drives." *New York Times*, 18 November 1987.

Haberman, Martin. "More Minority Teachers." *Phi Delta Kappan* 70, no. 10 (June 1989): 771–776.

Chapter 3

Grassmuck, Karen. "Columbia University Uses Philosophy of 'Selective Excellence' to Make Painful Cuts in Programs, Administration." *Chronicle of Higher Education* 36, no. 32 (25 April 1990): A1.

Chapter 4

Boulard, Garry A. "Higher Education Commissioners Urge State Systems to Limit Tuition Raises and to Explain Costs to Public." *Chronicle of Higher Education* 35, no. 4 (21 September 1988): A31.

"Fact File: Trends in Student Aid, 1980–81 to 1987–88." *Chronicle of Higher Education* 53, no. 4 (21 September 1988): A40.

Halstead, Kent. *Higher Education Tuition.* Washington, D.C.: Research Associates, 1989.

Hansen, Janet S. "Pay Now. Go Later." *College Board Review* 147 (Spring 1988): 8–10, 25–29.

"Higher Ed Groups Seek Increases in Student Aid." *Higher Education and National Affairs* 38, no. 9 (8 May 1989): 1.

Jaschik, Scott. "State-College Officials Call Public's Panic Over Fees Needless." *Chronicle of Higher Education* 34, no. 36 (18 May 1988): A1.

Leatherman, Courtney. "State Spending on Financial Aid for Needy Students Expected to Total $1.5 Billion This Academic Year." *Chronicle of Higher Education* 35, no. 24 (22 February 1989): A21, A27.

Murray, Troy. "Investment Issues." In *Invitational Conference on College Prepayment and Savings Plans: Proceedings.* New York: College Board, 1988.

"Opinion Leaders See Rising Costs as Major Concern." *Chronicle of Higher Education* 34, no. 24 (24 February 1988): A1.

"Students Cite Price as Deterrent to College." *Higher Education and National Affairs* 37, no. 18 (17 October 1988): 5, 8.

Trends in Student Aid: 1980 to 1990. Princeton, N. J.: College Entrance Examination Board, 1990.

Wilson, Robin. "Bennett's Tenure: Prominence for the Education Dept., but Alienation on Capitol Hill and the Campuses." *Chronicle of Higher Education* 35, no. 4 (21 September 1988): A24–25, A28.

Chapter 5

Bowen, Howard R., and Schuster, Jack H. *American Professors: A National Resource Imperiled.* New York: Oxford University Press, 1986.

Fiske, Edward B. "Lessons: Attracting Star Professors Starts Sounding Like the Bidding for Top Athletes." *New York Times*, 27 July 1988.

Foderaro, Lisa W. "Big Name on Campus." *New York Times*, 8 August 1988.

Lacey, Paul A. "Faculty Development and the Future of College Teaching." *New Directions for Teaching and Learning* 33 (Spring 1988): 57–69.

Mooney, Carolyn J. "Uncertainty is Rampant as Colleges Begin to Brace for Faculty Shortage Expected to Begin in 1990s." *Chronicle of Higher Education* 35, no. 20 (25 January 1989): A14-A17.

Sovern, Michael I. "Higher Education: The Real Crisis." *New York Times Magazine*, 22 January 1989.

Chapter 6

Carmody, Deirdre. "Colleges' S.A.T. Lists Can Be Creative Works." *New York Times*, 25 November 1987.

Sykes, Charles J. *Profscam: Professors and the Demise of Higher Education*. New York: Regnery Gateway, 1988.

Chapter 7

Berger, Joseph. "More Businesses and Schools Join to Attack Illiteracy in Workplace." *New York Times*, 8 September 1988.

Center for Policy Studies in Education, George Mason University. "Trends in Public School Budgets." Unpublished Report. Fairfax, Va.: Center for Policy Studies in Education, George Mason University, 1990.

Daniels, Lee A. "Illiteracy Seen as Threat to U.S. Economic Edge." *New York Times*, 7 September 1988.

Issues in Higher Education and Economic Development. Washington, D.C.: American Association of State Colleges and Universities, 1986.

"Practical Uses for Research Needed to Keep U.S. Competitive, Bok Says." *Higher Education & National Affairs* 38, no. 2 (30 January 1989): 1.

Chapter 8

Cage, Mary Crystal. "Tight Funds Thwarting States' Desire to Raise 2-Year-College Quality." *Chronicle of Higher Education* 36, no. 27 (21 March 1990): A1, A26.

Cohen, Arthur and Brawer, Florence. *The American Community College*. San Francisco: Jossey-Bass, 1989.

"Inbox." *Chronicle of Higher Education* 36, no. 27 (21 March 1990): A18.

Nazario, Sonia L. "Bearing the Brunt: Community Colleges Must Train Many of the Nation's Workers, But They May Not Be Up to the Job." *Wall Street Journal*, 9 February 1990.

Parnell, Dale. *Dateline 2000: The New Higher Education Agenda*. Washington, D.C.: Community College Press, 1990.

Templin, Robert. "Keeping the Door Open for Disadvantaged Students." In *Issues for Community College Leaders in a New Era*, edited by George B. Vaughan. San Francisco: Jossey-Bass, 1983.

Vaughan, George B. *Leadership in Transition: The Community College Presidency*. New York: ACE/Macmillan, 1989.

———. *Pathway to the Presidency: The Community College Dean of Instruction*. Washington, D.C.: Community College Press, 1990.

Walker, Rob. "Graying of Professors Said to Pose Challenge." *Richmond Times-Dispatch*, 13 March 1990.

Chapter 9

Gilley, J. Wade, and Fulmer, Kenneth A. *A Question of Leadership: or, To Whom Are the Governors Listening?* Unpublished Report. Fairfax, Va.: Center for Policy Studies in Education, George Mason University.

Rosenzweig, Robert. "Seeing Ourselves as Others See Us." *Chronicle of Higher Education* 33, no. 10 (6 November 1986): 104.

Schwartz, Amy. "A New Ivory Tower." *Washington Post* (8 November 1986): 22.

Chapter 10

Aldrich, Hope. "The Day the PTA Stayed Home," *Washington Monthly* 16, no. 5 (June 1984): 48.

Alexander, Lamar. "Master Teachers in Tennessee Schools." *American Educator* VII (Winter 1983): 12–14, 42.

———. Inaugural Address, 15 January 1983. In *Tennessee Blue Book 1983–1984*. Nashville: State of Tennessee, 1983.

———. "Time for Results: An Overview." *Phi Delta Kappan* 68 (November 1986): 202–204.

"Alexander on Education: The Views of Former Governor, Bush Adviser, and Soon-to-Be University Chief." *Chronicle of Higher Education* 34, no. 39 (8 June 1988): A16.

Birk, Ed. "TaxWatch Says Florida Ranks 13th in Per-Pupil Spending." *Tampa Tribune*, 13 March 1986.

Blumenstyk, Goldie. "Governor of Arkansas Faces Tough Battle with Legislature in Crusade to Raise Taxes for Renewal of Higher Education." *Chronicle of Higher Education* 35, no. 20 (25 January 1989): A21–22.

Bob Graham, The 38th Governor of Florida. Tallahassee: State of Florida, Office of the Governor, 1986.

Clinton, Bill. "Who Will Manage the Schools?" *Phi Delta Kappan* 68 (November 1986): 208–210.

Education Report Card: A Review of Florida's Accomplishments. Tallahassee: State of Florida, 1985.

"Florida Ranked No. 1 in Improving Public Education." *Tampa Tribune*, 13 May 1984.

Graham, Robert. "The State Role." *Journal of Education Finance* 8 (1982): 135–37.

Jaschik, Scott. "A Governor Pours Millions More into Education." *Chronicle of Higher Education* 33, no. 1 (3 September 1986): 25.

Kean, Thomas H. "What States Should Do (and Not Do) to Improve Undergraduate Education." *Chronicle of Higher Education* 31, no. 2 (11 September 1985): 128.

———. "Time for Action: A New Political Consensus." *Change* 18, no. 5 (September-October 1986): 10.

———. "Who Will Teach?" *Phi Delta Kappan* 68 (November 1986): 205–207.

Mooney, Carolyn J. "New Jersey's Kean Embraces Higher-Education Issues with Rare Passion." *Chronicle of Higher Education* 34, no. 7 (14 October 1987): A21, A28.

———. "No Joke: Higher Education in New Jersey Thrives Along with State's Booming Economy." *Chronicle of Higher Education* 34, no. 7 (14 October 1987): A20–29.

New Jersey's Design for Educational Excellence: Into the 21st Century. Trenton: New Jersey State Department of Education, 1988.

Newman, Frank. "Rising Expectations: Can States Help Renew Quality?" *Change* 17, no. 6 (November-December 1985): 12–15.

Osborne, David. *Laboratories of Democracy: A New Breed of Governor Creates Models for National Growth*. Boston: Harvard Business School Press, 1988.

Parish, John. "Excellence in Education: Tennessee's 'Master' Plan." *Phi Delta Kappan* 64 (June 1983): 722–724.

Pate-Bain, Helen. "A Teacher's Point of View on the Tennessee Master Teacher Plan." *Phi Delta Kappan* 64 (June 1983): 725–726.

Quest for Excellence: The Master Plan of the State University System of Florida. Tallahassee: State University System of Florida, 1985.

State of Arkansas, Office of the Governor. *The Alexander Report*. Little Rock: State of Arkansas, 1978.

"Teacher's Union Endorses Graham for U.S. Senate." *Tallahassee Democrat*, 23 June 1986.

Tifft, Susan "How to Tackle School Reform." *Time* 134, no. 2, (14 August 1989): 46–47.

University of Tennessee, Office of the President, 1990.

Wissner, Sheila. "Higher Education Enjoys 'Golden Era.'" *Nashville Tennessean*, 31 December 1989.

Chapter 12

Mills, D. Quinn. Conversation with the Author, Cambridge, Mass., 2 June 1989.

"The Worst Thing Is to Modernize." *U. S. News and World Report* 102, no. 4 (2 February 1987): 23.

Chapter 14

Alfred, Richard L., and Weissman, Julie. *Higher Education and the Public Trust: Improving Stature in Colleges and Universities.* ASHE-ERIC Higher Education Report No. 6. Washington, D.C.: Association for the Study of Higher Education, 1987.

Chapter 15

Cevero, R. *Suburban Gridlock.* New Brunswick, N.J.: Rutgers University, Center for Urban Policy Research, 1986.

————. *America's Suburban Centers: A Study of the Land-Use Transportation Link.* Final Report, U.S. Department of Transportation, Technology Sharing Program, DOT-T–88–14. Washington, D.C.: U.S. Department of Transportation, 1988.

Dentzer, S., McCormick, J., and Raine, G. "Back to the Suburbs." *Newsweek* 107, no. 16 (21 April 1986): 60–62.

Duncan, J. W. "The Role of the Information Industry in the Economy." *Bulletin of the American Society for Information Science* (February-March 1988): 16–17.

Erickson, R. A. "The Evolution of the Suburban Space Economy." *Urban Geography* 4 (1983): 95–121.

Fink, I., and Walker, D. "Campus Dispersal: Planning for the Location and Relocation of University Facilities." *Planning for Higher Education* 13, no. 1 (Fall 1984): 1–18.

Hartshorn, T. A., and Muller, P. O. *Suburban Business Centers: Employment Implications.* Final report, Project No. RED–808–G–84–5. Washington, D.C.: U.S. Department of Commerce, Economic Development Administration, 1986.

————. "Suburban Downtowns and the Transformation of Metropolitan Atlanta's Business Landscape." *Urban Geography* 10 (1989): 375–395.

Lambrecht, P. S. "Future Trends: Their Impact upon Higher Education Institutions." *Planning for Higher Education* 13, no. 1 (Fall 1984): 19–22.

La Tourette, J. E. "New Methods of Relating the University to Its Region." Presentation to the presidents of AASCU doctoral granting institutions. Washington, D.C., 6 June 1988.

Leinberger, C. B. "New Shape of Cities Will Impact Corporate Locations." *National Real Estate Investor* 26, no. 14 (December 1984): 40, 140.

———. "The Six Types of Urban Village Cores." *Urban Land* 47 (1988): 24–47.

Leinberger, C. B., and Lockwood, C. "How Business Is Reshaping America." *Atlantic Monthly* 258, no. 4 (October 1986): 43–52.

Malecki, E. J. "Hope or Hyperbole? High Tech and Economic Development." *Technology Review* 90, no. 7 (October 1987): 45–51.

McNulty, R. H. "Pollyanna, or Is the Glass Half Full?" *Annals of the American Academy* 488 (November 1986): 148–156.

Metropolitan Washington Council of Governments (COG). *Economic Trends in Metropolitan Washington, 1960–1989.* Washington, D.C.: Metropolitan Washington Council of Governments (COG), 1987.

The Office Network. *1989 International Office Market Report.* Washington, D.C.: Office Network, 1989.

Pearlstein, S. "Hot Spots: INC.'s List of the 50 Fastest-Growing U.S. Cities." *INC.* 9, no. 4 (April 1987): 50–52.

Rossini, F. A. "Earthnet: The University of the Future." *Technological Forecasting and Social Change* 26 (1984): 198–94.

Webb, A. "Los Angeles Comes of Age." *Atlantic Monthly* 261, no. 1 (January 1988): 31–56.

Worthy, F. S. "Booming American Cities." *Fortune* 116, no. 4 (17 August 1987): 30–37.

Chapter 17

Bush, Vannevar. "As We May Think." *Atlantic Monthly* (July 1945).

Index